FATTY LIV
DIET COOKBOOK
FOR BEGINNERS

1200 Days Of Healthy, Fast& Easy Recipes To Manage Your Weight And Liver, Regain Your Energy, Detox Your Body And Live a Healthy Life.| With 28-Day Meal Plan, Workout Plans And Good Habits To Start a New Lifestyle.

TRACY J. FREEMAN

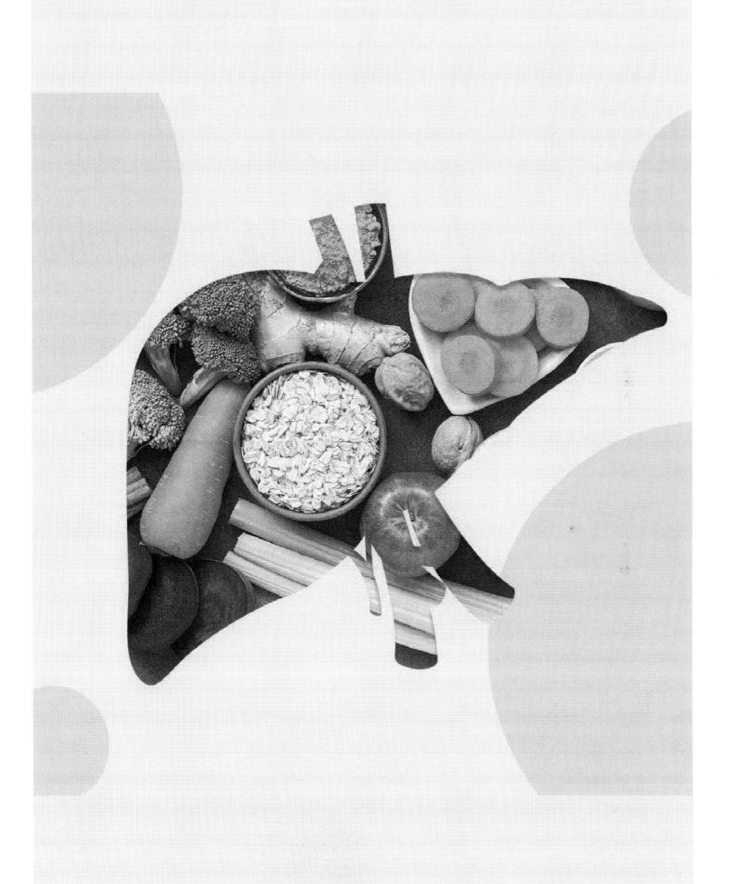

Table of Contents

Introduction

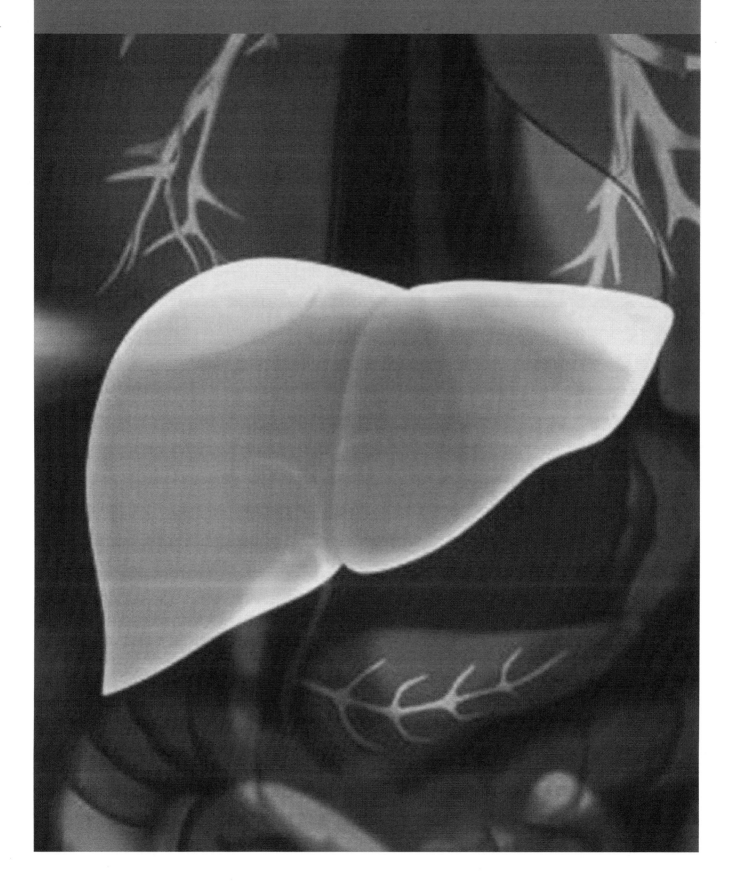

My name is Tracy Freeman, and about ten years ago, my journey with fatty liver diseases began. A sign that something was wrong was the results of a routine blood test for a life insurance policy. It showed elevated liver enzymes, which is a sign of fatty liver.

My physician at the time said that such a result was seen often and was no cause for worry. A short while after the tests, I experienced red spots and itchy skin often. When I went to see a different doctor, I was informed that there was a chance I had fatty liver disease. After further testing, it was conclusively shown that I did, in fact, have it.

Non-Alcoholic Fatty Liver Disease is a condition that leads to excess fat being stored in the liver. It does not involve any liver inflammation or cell damage. However, if left unchecked, it could worsen into a more severe form where there is liver inflammation and cell damage. It leads to liver scarring and, eventually, liver cirrhosis. At that point, you would need a new liver.

After my diagnosis, I knew I could not continue living as I did. I had to make fundamental changes to my diet, lifestyle, exercise routine, and outlook on life. At the time, my youngest child was eight years old, and I knew I had to make changes if I ever wanted to live to see my grandkids. I would deny my children the opportunity to grow with their mother beside them to guide them in life. After carefully examining all my options, I knew it would not be easy. However, I was ready for the tough journey ahead.

Chapter 1
Understanding Fatty Liver Disease

A diagnosis of advanced non-alcoholic fatty liver disease was first made in 1980. It confirmed that liver disease, which leads to an accumulation of fat, could develop in people who were not alcoholics. NAFLD is set to be the leading cause of liver disease globally. It is preventable and closely linked with type 2 diabetes, obesity, lifestyle, and diet. The condition afflicts around 30% of people in the US and Europe.

The liver is a large, red-brown organ located on the right side of the abdomen. It is a vital organ controlling hundreds of body functions, including digestion. One of the critical products of the liver is bile, which breaks down fat. It is also crucial to break down toxic compounds like alcohol and medication for excretion from the body. If its cells are damaged, the liver can repair itself.

In the initial stages, it is possible to reverse the condition. However, as the condition progresses, it impairs the liver's ability to self-repair. In the last stages, it usually turns into cirrhosis, which can cause liver failure. At this stage, the only treatment is a liver transplant.

A major concern with the conditions is that symptoms are absent in the first stages. However, some symptoms can appear as it develops. The main risk factors are alcohol consumption, high body weight, diabetes, pre-diabetes, high sugar diet, low physical activity, digestive problems, and genetic predisposition.

To diagnose fatty liver, one needs to undergo excessive testing, which includes blood tests, imaging tests, and liver function tests. Doctors will also ask about your exercise regime, weight, diet, and alcohol intake. One is considered to have fatty liver when over 5% of the liver is fat by weight.

Physical Exercises to Beat Fatty Liver

One of the most effective weapons against fatty liver is physical exercise. When most people think of exercise, they imagine a sweaty regime that involves excessive exhaustion. However, that is not the case.

Simple exercises are extremely effective against the condition. For instance, every 1000 steps could cut your chances of getting fatty liver by up to 0.87%. For most people, walking is something they can manage to do. You could start with short walks at your local park and pick up the pace as you get used to it. Besides walking, you can try the following exercises:

LIFT WEIGHTS

The common misconception is that only cardio can help cut weight. However, weight training is also important. When one lifts weights, it boosts metabolism, which helps you burn more calories. The body continually burns calories long after the workout. Lifting weights also helps to strengthen the tendons and muscles, which reduces the risk of injury during cardio. For it to be effective, you must carry out at least two sessions of 30 minutes each week. The process is gradual, and it won't be easy to see results.

SWIMMING

Swimming is an effective method of ridding the body of excess weight. The water helps to make the body feel light. At the same time, it helps to alleviate pressure on the knees and other joints, which makes it easy to exercise.

CYCLING

Cycling is also great for losing weight. A low-impact exercise does not strain the joints. Whether a stationary machine or a bike on the road, it can help you to stay healthy.

STRETCHING

Stretching is also important when working out. It helps to reduce the risk of injury to muscles when working out. At first, it can be difficult since the muscles are tight. Gently work up to the final goal of stretching them. Eventually, they will stretch out, and you will enjoy your workouts.

YOGA

While yoga is often used to relieve stress, it is also good exercise. It burns calories, which can help to cut weight. Taking part in two yoga classes of 90 minutes per week can help to reduce body weight. Yoga is also important in helping build mental resilience, which is needed to make other lifestyle changes to reverse fatty liver.

LIFESTYLE CHANGES TO BEAT FATTY LIVER

The liver is crucial for normal body function. Everything that goes into your body interacts with the liver in some form. To beat fatty liver, you will thus need to change your entire outlook on life. It is tough but possible. In the best-case scenario, the alternative is ending up on the operating table and getting your liver cut out.

LIMIT ALCOHOL

Alcoholism can cause alcoholic-fatty liver disease. However, even in the absence or moderate use of alcohol, you can still get fatty liver. When that happens, taking even moderate amounts of alcohol will make the situation worse. The only option is to limit alcohol intake or cut it out entirely.

EAT SMALL AND FREQUENTLY

If you are used to eating large meals in one go, this is the time to change. Start eating small portions every few hours to enhance your metabolism. With time, you will start losing weight. To heal the liver, you must lose weight. That means along with breakfast, lunch, and dinner, you will also have extra meals between them.

EAT ENOUGH PROTEIN

Eating enough protein is essential for boosting your metabolism. It is also useful in healing the liver. An adult needs around 1 gram of protein per kilo of weight. Most people who practice a vegetarian diet only meet a portion of this requirement. Ensure at least one protein source in all your minor and major meals. Some protein sources are lean meats, low-fat milk, soya, nuts, seeds, legumes, and pulses.

EAT MORE VEGETABLES AND FRUITS

Fruits and vegetables help boost fiber in your diet. Moreover, they can help heal the liver. Additionally, the fiber keeps you full, which is useful in fighting obesity. Green leafy vegetables and whole fruits are rich in antioxidants, which protect the liver cells from damage.

CONSUME HEALTHY FATS

Add food sources rich in Omega-3 monounsaturated fats to your diet. These fats help to cut hepatic lipids, which improves liver fat. Omega-3 fats are anti-inflammatory, which protect the liver from inflammation.

CUT SATURATED FATS

Saturated fats include ghee, butter, cheese, red meat, full-fat dairy products, and margarine. Consuming these fats will boost the deposits of fats in the liver. It is vital to eliminate them.

AVOID SUGARY FOODS

Sugary and fatty foods, especially processed ones like biscuits, mathi, samosa, jams, ketchup, and bread, are highly inflammatory. It is crucial to avoid them to boost the liver healing process.

HYDRATE

Water is crucial to metabolism. Without water, it is hard for the liver to break down chemicals and food molecules for absorption. Keep your body hydrated at all times. If you feel thirsty, do not deny your body some water.

HAVE MEALS ON FIXED TIMES

Food is the leading cause of fatty liver in young people especially. Eating without a schedule is to be avoided at all costs. Have major meals at fixed times, and then proceed to have minor meals in between at fixed times. At dinnertime, have a light meal to reduce the risk of developing advanced fatty liver.

SLEEP BETTER

If you sleep on a schedule, it will do wonders for your metabolism. It will help you achieve hormonal balance, which will help you cut stress and cut weight. Additionally, it balances ghrelin-leptin production, which is crucial for a healthy liver.

STOP SMOKING

Smoking not only damages your lungs, but it could also boost your chances of catching liver cancer. Besides that, it makes it harder for the liver to function, which could make it harder to repair itself. If you have never smoked tobacco, do not start. If you have fatty liver, using tobacco in any form will not help your condition.

GET VACCINATED

If you have fatty liver, vaccinate for hepatitis A and B, both viral liver diseases. To avoid Hepatitis A, do not eat raw seafood or shellfish. Hepatitis B can be contracted via unprotected sex, contaminated needles, and exposure to infected blood. If you do not get the Hepatitis B vaccine, ensure you engage in safe sex. Once you contract hepatitis, it is incurable, albeit manageable. However, it could exacerbate the condition.

BE CAREFUL OF TRADITIONAL REMEDIES

Once you have a fatty liver, it can be easy to believe that you can simply pop some traditional medicine, which promise results in days or weeks. Most of these remedies are unregulated, and they contain toxins. When taken, they increase stress on the liver, which could hinder the liver in its normal functions. They can cause liver inflammation and irreversible liver damage. Sometimes leading to liver failure.

AVOID FAD DIETS AND WEIGHT LOSS PILLS

Weight-loss pills bought over the counter are not going to cure fatty liver. Sometimes, they contain harmful ingredients that could harm the liver. Besides pills, there are fad diets that promise results in days.

Any diet that has the potential to change your body weight fast will also damage your liver. If you have to make dietary changes that leave you feeling dizzy and disoriented, it will harm your liver. These diets often lack essential nutrients needed to maintain normal body function.

An example of a fad diet is a liver detox cleanse diet. Contrary to belief, no diet can cleanse the liver. Healing the liver requires a whole-body approach that improves your overall health.

COUNT YOUR CARBS

One of the most significant risk factors for fatty liver is obesity. To begin dealing with obesity, you must reduce your carbs intake. In short, obesity is caused by taking in more carbohydrates than your body uses. The balance is stored in your body as fat, which leads to obesity over time. Counting your carbs can help to prevent obesity and reduce your weight. Below are tips on how to count your carbs and fight fatty liver the right way.

READ THE FOOD LABELS

Most food items at the local store have nutritional labels. Ensure that you check the serving size. Some food packages have more servings than you would imagine. If you are eating out, call ahead or check their site. Ask if the menu contains nutritional facts. Many restaurants today show you nutritional information.

CHECK OUT REFERENCE BOOKS, SITES, AND APPS

In the information age, finding out about carb counts is quite easy. Today, some apps can help to calculate the carb count. You can tell exactly how many carbs you consume per serving in a few minutes.

MAINTAIN A FOOD JOURNAL

Creating a food journal may seem like a lot of work. However, it will take less time and effort that would be needed to get a new liver if your current one fails. Work on creating a journal of everything you eat and your carb count.

It can be an online journal or a physical book. It could also be a convenient app on your phone. Write down what you eat for breakfast, lunch, snacks, and supper. Think about your portions, and look at the carb count for the portions. If you need to know the portion size, start measuring the food and noting the portions. Combine foods into meals, and add up the carb count. Over time, you will have a better sense of your carbs consumption.

USE MEASURING CUPS

One way to check your portion size is to use measuring cups. If the serving is one cup, you use one cup to tell how much you eat. If you want to cut your serving in half, measure half a cup. If you do not have a measuring cup, use your hands instead.

A fist is about one cup big. The palm is about three ounces, and the thumb is about one ounce or one tablespoon. The thumb tip is about a teaspoon, while a handful is around half a cup. However, this is just an estimate if you still need the cup. For the best results, ensure you get yourself a measuring cup.

GET A FOOD SCALE

Fresh foods, like vegetables, potatoes, and apples, come in varying sizes. In most instances, there are no nutritional labels. A large and small fruit can have a weight difference of up to 20 grams. Weigh the fresh foods and check the carb count. Small scales cost two to five dollars and will serve you for a long time. Once you can accurately measure how much goes into your body, you can make the proper adjustments.

PRACTICE AND HAVE FUN

Carb counting is a bit more complex than reading the food label. A long process that will entail measuring everything that goes into your belly. As you practice, you will get good at it. Always keep in mind that fighting fatty liver is not an overnight story. It is a journey that will last your whole life. That means you will have the rest of your life to perfect carb counting.

What Else to Fight Fatty Liver Disease?

MEDICATION

There is no FDA-approved fatty liver medication. However, doctors often prescribe medication to treat other illnesses like type 2 diabetes and high cholesterol. Always speak to a physician about managing conditions that could exacerbate fatty liver.

GO OUTDOORS

Even without exercising, going outdoors can enhance insulin sensitivity, which is good for fighting fatty liver. You do not need to be doing a specific activity; you need to be mobile, doing simple chores. This could include visiting friends, parks, dog walking, and other menial tasks.

KEEP UP WITH YOUR DOCTOR'S APPOINTMENTS

Early detection and management is the best way to reverse fatty liver. As soon as you get a positive diagnosis, do not feel sorry for yourself. It would help if you made changes immediately. The easiest to make is to reduce sugar and alcohol intake. You should also significantly reduce smoking and tobacco use if you hope to save your life.

CHANGES DO WORK

The good news with fatty liver is that lifestyle changes do work. You can join an online support group for extra encouragement. Those who have fatty livers have not been handed a death sentence. If caught early, it is a warning from your body that you are not headed in the right direction. While it is a serious warning, it is possible to make important changes to remain healthy. Millions of people worldwide have been saved by lifestyle changes to combat fatty liver. The liver is extremely resilient, and when given the proper assistance, it can do wonders.

FOOD MATTERS

When it comes to food choices, the goal is to cut down on carbs. However, you also need to ensure you are getting all the proper nutrients, such as Vitamin E and Omega-3, and Vitamin D. Besides these three, numerous micronutrients are needed to restore your body and liver to their proper place.

However, many need more resources or knowledge to find the right meals that help them stay healthy and happy. Eating right can be different from eating boring. You can enjoy tasty meals and feel full and happy while being healthy.

In this cookbook, I have detailed recipes I have developed over the years in my long journey with fatty liver. At first, I thought that eating healthy meant I would never enjoy another meal in my life. I thought I would be stuck eating bland food like that served in hospitals.

However, the personal drive I had to stay healthy, and my desire to ensure my family and I could still enjoy dinner together, led me to create these wonderful recipes. They have served us over the years and helped me significantly progress in reversing my fatty liver. If you try them for yourself, you, too, could begin the journey back to full health and happiness.

The recipes are simple, and the ingredients are adaptable while remaining healthy and delicious. No matter the season of the year, or your locality, you can find a recipe that works for you. With so many options to pick from, you can pick meals at random until you find something that works for you. You can work together to come up with creative recipes of your own based on the ones in this cookbook. The goal of this cookbook is to make eating healthy fun and delicious. If you do not get it right at first, there are always opportunities to try something else.

Begin your journey to reverse fatty liver with these recipes. Try them yourself today!

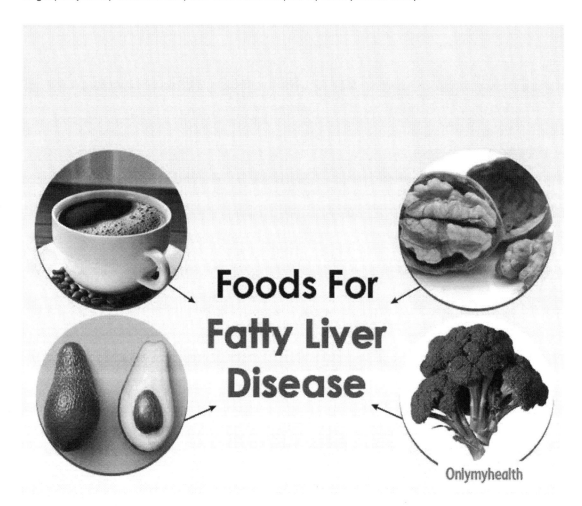

Foods For Fatty Liver Disease

Onlymyhealth

Week 1

Here is the following first week's meal plan for the fatty liver diet. Try to follow the plan thoroughly to start getting the benefits of it.

Meal Plan	Breakfast	Lunch	Dinner	Snack
Day-1	Pickled Red Cabbage	Grilled Basil-lemon Tofu Burgers	Kidney Bean and Parsley-lemon Salad	Oatmeal Cookies
Day-2	Nectarine Pancakes	Artichoke Feta Penne	Chicken and Lemongrass Sauce	Trail Mix
Day-3	Green Salad with Herbs	Cajun Garlic Shrimp Noodle Bowl	Chicken and Semolina Meatballs	Zucchini Cakes
Day-4	Pickled Red Cabbage	Avocado Boat with Salsa	Quinoa & Black Bean Stuffed Sweet Potatoes	Yogurt Dip
Day-5	Toasted Crostini	Grilled Basil-lemon Tofu Burgers	Bulgur and Chicken Skillet	Cucumber-basil Salsa On Halibut Pouches
Day-6	Mexican Style Burritos	Cream Cheese Artichoke Mix	Beef Dish	Feta Tomato Sea Bass
Day-7	Keto Egg Fast Snickerdoodle Crepes	White Bean Soup	Bell Peppers On Chicken Breasts	Jalapeno Chickpea Hummus

Week 2

Here is the following second week's meal plan for the fatty liver diet. It's the second stage of the 4 weeks meal plan that you must take into account carefully.

Meal Plan	Breakfast	Lunch	Dinner	Snack
Day-1	Olive Frittata	Meat Cakes	Meat Cakes	Eggplant Dip
Day-2	Nectarine Pancakes	Leek, Bacon and Pea Risotto	Smoked Salmon and Watercress Salad	Avocado Dip
Day-3	Pumpkin Coconut Oatmeal	Moules Marinieres	Turkey and Chick-peas	Chicken Bites
Day-4	Green Salad with Herbs	Tuna Noodle Casserole	White Bean Soup	Chicken Bites
Day-5	Olive Frittata	Steamed Mussels with Coconut-Curry	Chicken Breast & Zucchini Linguine	Lime Pea Guacamole
Day-6	Pancakes	Cod and Mushrooms Mix	Balsamic Steak with Feta, Tomato, and Basil	Lime Pea Guacamole
Day-7	Cauliflower Cous-cous Salad	Salmon Burgers	Ginger Chicken Drumsticks	Lemon Swordfish

Week 3

Here is the following third week's meal plan for the fatty liver diet. In this stage, you already got the result of the previous two weeks' diet plan. So, follow this third stage of the meal plan completely to get a better result.

Meal Plan	Breakfast	Lunch	Dinner	Snack
Day-1	Spinach Wrap	Zucchini and Mozzarella Casserole	Miso-Glazed Salmon	Honey Garlic Shrimp
Day-2	Detox Porridge	Seared Scallops	California Poke Bowl	Lime Pea Guacamole
Day-3	Papaya Juice	Provencal Summer Salad	Tasty Beef Stew	Lemon Swordfish
Day-4	Nectarine Pancakes	Black Cod	Turkey and Quinoa Stuffed Peppers	Red Pepper Tapenade
Day-5	Blue Breeze Shake	Roasted Vegetable Salad	Salmon Pasta	Plum Wraps
Day-6	Turkey and Spinach Scramble on Melba Toast	Spanish Tomato Salad	Sautéed Cauliflower Delight	Feta and Roasted Red Pepper Bruschetta
Day-7	Beetroot & Parsley Smoothie	Grilled Salmon Summer Salad	Salmon & Arugula Salad	Crunchy Veggie Chips

Week 4

This is the final stage of our 4 week's fatty liver diet meal plan. In this stage, you already have formed a habit of maintaining a fatty liver diet. So, follow this final stage to get best the best result in your body and mind.

Meal Plan	Breakfast	Lunch	Dinner	Snack
Day-1	Green Salad with Herbs	Wild Rice Prawn Salad	Buckwheat and Grapefruit Porridge	Oatmeal Energy Balls
Day-2	Mediterranean Egg Casserole	Crunchy Veggie Chips	Chicken and Lemongrass Sauce	Zucchini Fritters
Day-3	Nectarine Pancakes	Cherry Berry Bulgur Bowl	Lemony Lamb and Potatoes	Zucchini Fritters
Day-4	Spinach Wrap	Raspberry Overnight Porridge	Crunchy Veggie Chips	Yogurt Dip
Day-5	Beets Omelette	Baked Curried Apple Oatmeal Cups	Lemony Lamb and Potatoes	Zucchini Cakes
Day-6	Watermelon Drink	Crunchy Quinoa Meal	Banana Quinoa	
Day-7	Glory Smoothie	Vegetable Platter with Tzatziki Dip	Roasted Buffalo Chickpeas	Eggplant Dip

Chapter 3
Homemade Staples

Pickled Red Cabbage

Prep time: 15 minutes, plus 2 or more hours pickling time | Serves 8

- 1 small head red cabbage, shredded
- ¼ cup apple cider vinegar
- Juice of 1 lime
- 1 tablespoon maple syrup or honey
- ½ teaspoon sea salt

1. Place the cabbage, vinegar, lime juice, maple syrup, and salt in a large container and toss to coat.
2. Cover and refrigerate until the cabbage softens, tossing occasionally, about 2 hours.
3. Refrigerate in the container for up to 1 week.

PER SERVING

Calories: 31; Protein: 1g; Total Fat: 0g; Total Carbohydrates: 7g; Fiber: 2g; Sugars: 4g; Sodium: 93mg; Iron: 1mg

Creamy Caesar Dressing

Prep time: 10 minutes | Makes: about 1½ cups

- 1 cup plain low-fat Greek yogurt
- Juice of 1 lemon
- 3 tablespoons grated Parmesan cheese
- 1 tablespoon extra-virgin olive oil
- 1 tablespoon Worcestershire sauce
- 2 teaspoons minced garlic
- Sea salt
- Freshly ground black pepper

1. In a small container, combine the yogurt, lemon juice, Parmesan cheese, oil, Worcestershire sauce, garlic, salt, and pepper until blended.
2. Refrigerate for up to 1 week.

PER SERVING (¼ CUP)

Calories: 61; Protein: 3g; Total Fat: 4g; Total Carbohydrates: 5g; Fiber: 0g; Sugars: 3g; Sodium: 128mg; Iron: 0mg

Balsamic Honey Dressing

Prep time: 10 minutes | Makes: about 1 cup

- ¼ cup balsamic vinegar
- 1 tablespoon honey
- 1 tablespoon Dijon mustard
- 1 teaspoon chopped fresh thyme
- ½ cup extra-virgin olive oil
- Sea salt
- Freshly ground black pepper

1. In a small bowl, whisk the vinegar, honey, mustard, and thyme until blended.
2. Whisk in the oil in a thin stream until the dressing is emulsified. Season with salt and pepper.
3. Refrigerate in a sealed container for up to 1 week.

PER SERVING (2 TABLESPOONS)

Calories: 136; Protein: 0g; Total Fat: 14g; Total Carbohydrates: 4g; Fiber: 0g; Sugars: 3g; Sodium: 43mg; Iron: 0mg

Smoky Barbecue Sauce

Prep time: 5 minutes | Cook time: 15 minutes | Makes: about 2 cups

- 1 cup water
- 1 (12-ounce) can no-salt-added tomato paste
- ⅓ cup apple cider vinegar
- 2 tablespoons maple syrup or honey
- 2 tablespoons Worcestershire sauce
- 1 tablespoon smoked paprika
- ½ tablespoon garlic powder
- ½ teaspoon onion powder
- ½ teaspoon chili powder
- ½ teaspoon sea salt

1. In a medium saucepan, whisk the water, tomato paste, vinegar, maple syrup, Worcestershire sauce, paprika, garlic powder, onion powder, chili powder, and salt until blended.
2. Bring the mixture to a low boil on medium-high heat. Reduce the heat to low, and simmer, stirring frequently until slightly thickened, about 15 minutes.
3. Cool and refrigerate in a sealed container for up to 1 week.

PER SERVING (¼ CUP)

Calories: 59; Protein: 2g; Total Fat: 0g; Total Carbohydrates: 13g; Fiber: 2g; Sugars: 9g; Sodium: 147mg; Iron: 2mg

Tzatziki Sauce

Prep time: 15 minutes | Serves 8

- 1 large English cucumber
- 2 cups low-fat plain Greek yogurt or nondairy yogurt
- 2 tablespoons chopped fresh dill
- Juice of ½ lemon
- 1½ teaspoons minced garlic
- Sea salt
- Freshly ground black pepper

1. Using the small hole side of a box grater, grate the cucumber onto a clean kitchen cloth. Wring the grated cucumber until as much liquid is removed as possible, and transfer it to a medium bowl.
2. Add the yogurt, dill, lemon juice, and garlic, and stir until combined. Season with salt and pepper.
3. Refrigerate in a sealed container for up to 5 days.

PER SERVING (¼ CUP)

Calories: 46; Protein: 4g; Total Fat: 1g; Total Carbohydrates: 6g; Fiber: 0g; Sugars: 5g; Sodium: 63mg; Iron: 0mg

Basil Spinach Pesto

Prep time: 10 minutes | Makes: about 2 cups

- 2 cups fresh basil leaves
- 1 cup baby spinach
- 4 garlic cloves, smashed
- ¼ cup pine nuts
- ¼ cup grated Parmesan cheese (optional)
- ½ cup extra-virgin olive oil
- Sea salt
- Freshly ground black pepper

1. Place the basil, spinach, garlic, pine nuts, and Parmesan cheese (if using) in a blender and pulse until the mixture is pureed, scraping down the sides once.
2. While the blender is running, add the olive oil in a thin stream and process until the pesto is smooth. Season with salt and pepper.
3. Refrigerate in a sealed container for up to 2 weeks.

PER SERVING (2 TABLESPOONS)

Calories: 83; Protein: 1g; Total Fat: 9g; Total Carbohydrates: 1g; Fiber: 0g; Sugars: 0g; Sodium: 40mg; Iron: 0mg

Eggplant Tomato Sauce

Prep time: 10 minutes | Cook time: 30 minutes | Serves 6

- 2 tablespoons extra-virgin olive oil
- 1 small eggplant, peeled and cut into ½-inch chunks (about 3 cups)
- 1 onion, chopped
- 1 tablespoon minced garlic
- 1 (28-ounce) can low-sodium diced tomatoes, undrained
- 1 (6-ounce) can no-salt-added tomato paste
- ¼ cup vegetable broth or water
- ¼ cup chopped fresh basil
- 3 tablespoons chopped fresh parsley
- Sea salt
- Freshly ground black pepper

1. Heat the oil in a large pot over medium-high heat and sauté the eggplant, onion, and garlic until softened and lightly browned, about 10 minutes.
2. Add the tomatoes, tomato paste, and broth, and bring the mixture to a boil. Reduce the heat to low, partially cover, and simmer for about 15 minutes until the veggies are very tender.
3. Add the basil and parsley and simmer for 5 minutes. Remove the sauce from the heat and season with salt and pepper.
4. Serve immediately or cool and refrigerate in a sealed container for up to 1 week.

PER SERVING (1 CUP)

Calories: 117; Protein: 4g; Total Fat: 5g; Total Carbohydrates: 18g; Fiber: 7g; Sugars: 11g; Sodium: 60mg; Iron: 2mg

Mediterranean Spice Rub

Prep time: 5 minutes | Makes: about ¼ cup

- 2 tablespoons dried oregano
- 2 teaspoons dried basil
- ½ tablespoon dried thyme
- 1 teaspoon garlic powder
- 1 teaspoon paprika
- ½ teaspoon ground black pepper
- ½ teaspoon cumin

1. Mix the oregano, basil, thyme, garlic powder, paprika, pepper, and cumin in a small container and store at room temperature for up to 1 month.

PER SERVING (1 TEASPOON)

Calories: 4; Protein: 0g; Total Fat: 0g; Total Carbohydrates: 1g; Fiber: 0g; Sugars: 0g; Sodium: 1mg; Iron: 0mg

Sweet Potato Hummus

Prep time: 15 minutes| Serves 6

- 1 cup mashed, cooked sweet potato
- 1 cup canned chickpeas
- ¼ cup tahini
- Juice of 1 lemon
- 1 teaspoon minced garlic
- 2 tablespoons extra-virgin olive oil
- ½ teaspoon ground cumin
- Sea salt

1. Place the sweet potato, chickpeas, tahini, lemon juice, and garlic in a blender and blend until smooth.
2. Add the olive oil and cumin and blend until combined. Season with salt and pepper and serve, or refrigerate in a sealed container for up to 1 week.

PER SERVING (½ CUP)

Calories: 188; Protein: 5g; Total Fat: 11g; Total Carbohydrates: 20g; Fiber: 4g; Sugars: 4g; Sodium: 71mg; Iron: 2mg

Applesauce with Warm Spices

Prep time: 5 minutes | Cook time: 15 minutes | Serves 3

- 4 large apples, peeled, cored, and roughly chopped
- ¼ cup unsweetened apple juice or water
- Juice of ½ lemon
- 2 teaspoons ground cinnamon
- ½ teaspoon ground nutmeg
- ¼ teaspoon ground cloves

1. Place the apples, apple juice, lemon juice, cinnamon, nutmeg, and cloves in a medium saucepan over medium-high heat. Bring to a simmer, reduce the heat to low, partially cover, and simmer until the apples are very tender, about 15 minutes.
2. Remove the apples from the heat and use a potato masher to create the desired texture, or if you prefer very smooth applesauce, you can blend the mixture.
3. Cool and refrigerate in a sealed container for up to 5 days.

PER SERVING (1 CUP)

Calories: 156; Protein: 1g; Total Fat: 1g; Total Carbohydrates: 41g; Fiber: 5g; Sugars: 31g; Sodium: 2mg; Iron: 0mg

Basil Pesto

Prep time: 10 minutes | Makes 3½ cups

- 1 cup fresh basil leaves
- 1 cup fresh baby spinach leaves
- ½ cup freshly grated Parmesan cheese
- ½ cup extra-virgin olive oil
- ¼ cup pine nuts
- 4 garlic cloves, peeled
- ¼ teaspoon kosher or sea salt
- ¼ teaspoon freshly ground black pepper

1. In the bowl of a food processor, combine the basil, spinach, Parmesan cheese, olive oil, pine nuts, garlic, salt, and pepper and process until a paste forms, scraping down the sides of the bowl with a spatula as needed. Taste and adjust the seasoning, if necessary.
2. Store in airtight containers in the refrigerator for up to 5 days, or in the freezer for up to 2 months and thaw as needed. Or divide the pesto into ice cube trays, seal in a zip-top bag, and store in the freezer for up to 2 months. Pop pesto cubes out of the ice cube tray as needed.

PER SERVING (¼ CUP)

Calories: 102; Protein: 2g; Total fat: 10g; Total carbohydrates: 1g; Fiber: 0g; Sugars: 0g; Sodium: 89mg; Iron: 0mg

Homemade Turkey Breakfast Sausage

Prep time: 10 minutes | Cook time: 10 minutes | Makes 8

- 1 pound lean ground turkey
- ½ teaspoon salt
- ½ teaspoon ground sage
- ½ teaspoon dried thyme
- ½ teaspoon freshly ground black pepper
- ¼ teaspoon ground fennel seeds
- 1 teaspoon extra-virgin olive oil

1. In a large mixing bowl, combine the turkey, salt, sage, thyme, pepper, and fennel seeds. Mix well.
2. Shape the meat into eight small, round patties. Use this in recipes or cook as noted in the remaining steps and store for later.
3. In a skillet, heat the olive oil over medium-high heat. Cook the patties in the skillet for 3 to 4 minutes on each side until browned and cooked through.
4. Serve warm, or store in an airtight container in the refrigerator for up to 3 days or in the freezer for up to 1 month.

PER SERVING (1 PATTY)

Calories: 91; Protein: 11g; Total fat: 5g; Total carbohydrates: 0g; Fiber: 0g; Sugars: 0g; Sodium: 185mg; Iron: 1mg

Greek Lemon Vinaigrette
Prep time: 10 minutes | Makes 4

- ¼ cup red wine vinegar
- 3 garlic cloves, finely minced
- 2 tablespoons freshly squeezed lemon juice
- 2 tablespoons dried oregano
- 1 teaspoon Dijon mustard
- ¼ teaspoon sea salt
- ⅛ teaspoon freshly ground black pepper
- ¼ cup extra-virgin olive oil

1. In a small bowl, whisk together the red wine vinegar, garlic, lemon juice, oregano, mustard, salt, and pepper.
2. Pour in the olive oil in a thin stream, whisking constantly.
3. Store in a bottle in the refrigerator for up to 2 weeks. Shake before using.

PER SERVING (ABOUT 2 TABLESPOONS)
Calories: 132; Protein: 0g; Total fat: 14g; Total carbohydrates: 2g; Fiber: 1g; Sugars: 0g; Sodium: 94mg; Iron: 1mg

Mango Salsa
Prep time: 10 minutes, plus 20 minutes to rest | Makes 4

- 1 cup chopped fresh mango
- ½ red onion, diced
- ¼ cup chopped fresh cilantro
- 1 jalapeño pepper, seeded, ribs removed, and minced
- 1 garlic clove, finely minced
- Juice of 1 lime
- ½ teaspoon sea salt

1. In a small bowl, combine the mango, onion, cilantro, jalapeño, garlic, lime juice, and salt. Mix well.
2. Allow to sit at room temperature for about 20 minutes for the flavors to blend.
3. While this is best fresh, it can be stored tightly sealed in the refrigerator for up to 5 days.

PER SERVING (ABOUT ¼ CUP)
Calories: 35; Protein: 1g; Total fat: 0g; Total carbohydrates: 9g; Fiber: 1g; Sugars: 6g; Sodium: 147mg; Iron: 0mg

Guacamole
Prep time: 10 minutes | Makes 4

- 1 avocado, peeled, pitted, and cubed
- Juice of ½ lime
- 1 garlic clove, minced
- ¼ teaspoon sea salt
- ¼ red onion, finely minced
- ½ jalapeño pepper, seeded, ribs removed, and minced
- 2 tablespoons chopped fresh cilantro

1. In a small bowl, combine the avocado, lime juice, garlic, and salt.
2. Use a fork to mash the avocado and other ingredients until the desired consistency.
3. Stir in the onion, jalapeño, and cilantro.
4. Store in a small bowl or container. Place a layer of plastic wrap directly on the surface of the guacamole (rather than stretched over the top where air will be trapped) to keep it from browning, and then seal the container. It will keep this way in the refrigerator for up to 3 days.

PER SERVING (ABOUT ¼ CUP)
Calories: 86; Protein: 1g; Total fat: 7g; Total carbohydrates: 6g; Fiber: 4g; Sugars: 1g; Sodium: 82mg; Iron: 0mg

Chapter 4
Breakfast

Pan-fried Chicken with Oregano-orange Chimichurri & Arugula Salad

Prep time: 5 minutes | Cook time: 5 minutes| Serves 3

- 1 tablespoon orange juice
- 1 teaspoon orange zest
- 1 teaspoon dried oregano
- 1 small garlic clove, grated
- 2 teaspoon apple cider vinegar
- 1/2 cup chopped parsley
- 1 1/2 pound chicken, cut into 4 pieces
- 1 tablespoon lemon juice
- A pinch of pepper
- 1/4 cup olive oil
- 4 cups arugula
- 2 bulbs fennel, shaved
- 2 tablespoons whole-grain mustard

1. Make chimichurri: In a medium bowl, combine orange zest, oregano and garlic. Mix in vinegar, orange juice and parsley and then slowly whisk in ¼ cup of olive oil until emulsified. Season with black pepper.
2. Sprinkle the chicken with lemon juice and pepper; heat the remaining olive oil in a large skillet and cook the chicken over medium high heat for about 6 minutes per side or until browned.
3. Remove from heat and let rest for at least 10 minutes. Toss chicken, greens, and fennel with mustard in a medium bowl; season with salt and pepper.
4. Serve steak with chimichurri and salad. Enjoy!

PER SERVING

Carbs35 ,fat10g ,protein12g ,Calories 165

Red Pepper and Artichoke Frittata

Prep time: 10 minutes | Cook time: 20 minutes| Serves 2

- 4 large eggs
- 1 can (14-ounce) artichoke hearts, rinsed, coarsely chopped
- 1 medium red bell pepper, diced
- 1 teaspoon dried oregano
- 1/4 cup Parmesan cheese, freshly grated
- 1/4 teaspoon red pepper, crushed
- 1/4 teaspoon salt, or to taste
- 2 garlic cloves, minced
- 2 teaspoons extra-virgin olive oil, divided
- Freshly ground pepper, to taste

1. In a 10-inch non-stick skillet, heat 1 teaspoon of the olive oil over medium heat. Add the bell pepper; cook for about 2 minutes or until tender. Add the garlic and the red pepper; cook for about 30 seconds, stirring. Transfer the mixture to a plate and wipe the skillet clean.
2. In a medium mixing bowl, whisk the eggs. Stir in the artichokes, cheese, the bell pepper mixture, and season with salt and pepper.
3. Place an over rack 4 inches from the source of heat; preheat broiler.
4. Brush the skillet with the remaining 1 teaspoon olive oil and heat over medium heat. Pour the egg mixture into the skillet and tilt to evenly distribute. Reduce the heat to medium low; cook for about 3-4 minutes, lifting the edges to allow the uncooked egg to flow underneath, until the bottom of the frittata is light golden.
5. Transfer the pan into the broiler, cook for about 1 1/2-2 1/2 minutes, or until the top is set.
6. Slide into a platter; cut into wedges and serve

PER SERVING

Fat 18, sodium734 mg, carb18 g, fiber8 g, protein21 g

Nectarine Pancakes

Prep time: 10 minutes | Cook time: 30 minutes| Serves 4

- 1 cup whole wheat flour
- ¼ tsp baking soda
- ¼ tsp baking powder
- 1 cup nectarines
- 2 eggs
- 1 cup milk

1. In a bowl combine all ingredients together and mix well
2. In a skillet heat olive oil
3. Pour ¼ of the batter and cook each pancake for 1-2 minutes per side
4. When ready remove from heat and serve

PER SERVING

Carbs7g , fat14g, protein15g , Calories 210

Green Salad with Herbs

Prep time: 10 minutes | Cook time: 30 minutes| Serves 4

- 1 bunch rocket
- 2 baby cos, outer leaves discarded, roughly chopped
- 1 curly endive, outer leaves removed, roughly chopped
- 2 tablespoons chopped parsley
- 2 tablespoons chopped fresh dill
- 2 tablespoons snipped chives
- 1/2 cup extra-virgin olive oil
- 2 tablespoons fresh lemon juice

1. In a large bowl, mix rocket, cos and endive and herbs.
2. In another small bowl, whisk together olive oil, fresh lemon juice, salt and pepper until well blended; pour over the salad and toss to coat well. Serve.

PER SERVING

Calories 283.6, fat11.5g, carbs 31g , protein 10.9g

Pineapple, Macha & Beet Chia Pudding

Prep time: 10 minutes | Cook time: 10 minutes| Serves 4

- 1 cup chia seeds
- 1 teaspoon raw honey
- 2 cups almond milk
- 1 teaspoon matcha green tea powder
- 2 tablespoons fresh beetroot juice
- 1 whole pineapple
- 1 cup freshly squeezed lemon juice
- 1 knob of fresh ginger
- Toasted almonds and figs to serve

GREEN CHIA PUDDING LAYER:

1. Add another half each of chia seeds, raw honey, almond milk, and matcha green tea powder to the blender and until very smooth; transfer to a bowl.
2. Beetroot layer: blend together beetroot and ginger with the remaining chia seeds, raw honey, vanilla, and coconut milk until very smooth; transfer to a separate bowl. In a food processor, puree the fresh pineapple until fine.
3. To assemble, layer the chia pudding in the bottom of serving glasses, followed by the pureed pineapple and then the beetroot layer. Top with figs and toasted almonds for a crunchy finish.

Pancakes

Prep time: 10 minutes | Cook time: 30 minutes| Serves 4

- 1 cup whole wheat flour
- ¼ tsp baking soda
- ¼ tsp baking powder
- 2 eggs
- 1 cup milk

1. In a bowl combine all ingredients together and mix well.
2. In a skillet heat olive oil.
3. Pour ¼ of the batter and cook each pancake for 1-2 minutes per side.
4. When ready remove from heat and serve.

PER SERVING

Carbs2g, fat 6g , protein10g, Calories 100

Turkey and Spinach Scramble on Melba Toast

Prep time: 10 minutes | Cook time: 15 minutes| Serves 2

- Extra virgin olive oil – 1 teaspoon
- Raw spinach – 1 cup
- Garlic – ½ clove, minced
- Nutmeg – 1 teaspoon grated
- Cooked and diced turkey breast – 1 cup
- Melba toast – 4 slices
- Balsamic vinegar – 1 teaspoon

1. Heat a pot over a source of heat and add oil.
2. Add turkey and heat through for 6 to 8 minutes.
3. Add spinach, garlic, and nutmeg and stir-fry for 6 minutes more.
4. Plate up the Melba toast and top with spinach and turkey scramble.
5. Drizzle with balsamic vinegar and serve.

PER SERVING

Calories: 301 ,Fat: 19g ,Carb: 12g ,Phosphorus: 215mg ,Potassium: 269mg ,Sodium: 360mg ,Protein: 19g

Mediterranean Egg Casserole

Prep time: 10 minutes | Cook time: 50 minutes| Serves 4

- 1 1/2 cups (6 ounces) feta cheese, crumbled
- 1 jar (6 ounces) marinated artichoke hearts, drained well, coarsely chopped
- 10 eggs
- 2 cups milk, low-fat
- 2 cups fresh baby spinach, packed, coarsely chopped
- 6 cups whole-wheat baguette, cut into 1-inch cubes
- 1 tablespoon garlic (about 4 cloves), finely chopped
- 1 tablespoon olive oil, extra-virgin
- 1/2 cup red bell pepper, chopped
- 1/2 cup Parmesan cheese, shredded
- 1/2 teaspoon pepper
- 1/2 teaspoon red pepper flakes
- 1/2 teaspoon salt
- 1/3 cup kalamata olives, pitted, halved
- 1/4 cup red onion, chopped
- 1/4 cup tomatoes (sun-dried) in oil, drained, chopped

1. Preheat oven to 350F.
2. Grease a 9x13-inch baking dish with olive oil cooking spray.
3. In an 8-inch non-stick pan over medium heat, heat the olive oil. Add the onions, garlic, and bell pepper; cook for about 3 minutes, frequently stirring, until slightly softened. Add the spinach; cook for about 1 minute or until starting to wilt.
4. Layer half of the baguette cubes in the preparation ared baking dish, then 1 cup of the eta, 1/4 cup Parmesan, the bell pepper mix, artichokes, the olives, and the tomatoes. Top with the remaining baguette cubes and then with the remaining 1/2 cup of feta.
5. In a large mixing bowl, whisk the eggs and the low-fat milk together. Beat in the pepper, salt and the pepper. Pour the mix over the bread layer in the baking dish, slightly pressing down. Sprinkle with the remaining 1/4 cup Parmesan.
6. Bake for about 40-45 minutes, or until the center is set and the top is golden brown. Before serving, let stand for 15 minutes

PER SERVING

Cal360, total fat21 g, chol270 mg, sodium880 mg, carb 24 g, fiber3 g, sugar7 g, protein20 g

Toasted Crostini

Prep time: 10 minutes | Cook time: 15 minutes | Serves 4

- 12 slices (1/3-inch thick) whole-wheat baguette, toasted
- Coarse salt and freshly ground pepper
- For the spread:
- 1 can chickpeas (15 1/2 ounces), drained, rinsed
- 1/4 cup olive oil, extra-virgin
- 1 tablespoon lemon juice, freshly squeezed
- 1 small clove garlic, minced
- 2 tablespoons olive oil, extra-virgin, divided
- 2 tablespoons celery, finely diced, plus celery leaves for garnish
- 8 large green olives, pitted, cut into 1/8-inch slivers

1. In a food processor, combine the spread ingredients and season with salt and pepper; set aside.
2. In a small mixing bowl, combine 1 tablespoon of olive oil and the remaining ingredients. Season with salt and pepper. Set aside.
3. Divide the spread between the toasted baguette slices, top with the relish. Drizzle the remaining1 tablespoon of olive oil over each and season with pepper. If desired, garnish with the celery leaves. Serve immediately.

PER SERVING

Cal603, total fat3.7 g, sodium781 mg, carb 79.2 g, fiber6.8 g, sugar19.1 g, protein19.1 g

Pumpkin Coconut Oatmeal

Prep time: 10 minutes | Cook time: 15 minutes | Serves 6

- 2 cups oatmeal
- 1 cup of coconut milk
- 1 cup milk
- 1 teaspoon Pumpkin pie spices
- 2 tablespoons pumpkin puree
- 1 tablespoon Honey
- ½ teaspoon butter

1. Pour coconut milk and milk in the saucepan. Add butter and bring the liquid to boil.
2. Add oatmeal, stir well with the help of a spoon and close the lid.
3. Simmer the oatmeal for 7 minutes over the medium heat.
4. Meanwhile, mix up together honey, pumpkin pie spices, and pumpkin puree.
5. When the oatmeal is cooked, add pumpkin puree mixture and stir well.
6. Transfer the cooked breakfast in the serving plates.

PER SERVING

Calories 232, fat 12.5, fiber 3.8, carbs 26.2, protein 5.9

Cauliflower Couscous Salad

Prep time: 10 minutes | Cook time:25 minutes| Serves 4

- 1 large head cauliflower, cut into florets
- 3-4 green onions, thinly sliced
- 2 garlic cloves, finely minced
- 1 jalapeño, seeds and ribs removed, minced
- 1 cup shredded carrots
- 1 cup diced celery
- 1 cup diced cucumber
- 1 green apple, diced
- Juice of 1 lemon
- 1 tablespoon extra-virgin olive oil
- Sea salt
- Freshly ground black peppe

1. Using two batches, set your cauliflower to pulse in a food processor until finely chopped.
2. Transfer to a mixing bowl with the remaining ingredients then gently toss until combined.
3. Serve and enjoy.

PER SERVING

Carbs 3g,fat10g , protein12g , Calories 165

Spinach Wrap

Prep time: 10 minutes | Cook time: 10 minutes| Serves 4

- 4 pieces (10-inch) spinach wraps (or whole wheat tortilla or sun-dried tomato wraps)
- 1 pound chicken tenders
- 1 cup cucumber, chopped
- 3 tablespoons extra-virgin olive oil
- 1 medium tomato, chopped
- 1/3 cup couscous, whole-wheat
- 2 teaspoons garlic, minced
- 1/4 teaspoon salt, divided
- 1/4 cup lemon juice
- 1/2 cup water
- 1/2 cup fresh mint, chopped
- 1 cup fresh parsley, chopped

1. In a small saucepan, pour the water and bring to a boil. Stir in the couscous, remove pan from heat, cover, and allow to stand for 5 minutes, then fluff using a fork; set aside.
2. Meanwhile, in a small mixing bowl, combine the mint, parsley, oil, lemon juice, garlic, 1/8 teaspoon of the salt, and the pepper.
3. In a medium mixing bowl, toss the chicken with the 1 tablespoon of the mint mixture and the remaining 1/8 teaspoon of salt.
4. Place the chicken mixture into a large non-stick skillet; cook for about 3-5 minutes each side, or until heated through. Remove from the skillet, allow to cool enough to handle, and cut into bite-sized pieces.
5. Stir the remaining mint mixture, the cucumber, and the tomato into the couscous.
6. Spread about 3/4 cup of the couscous mix onto each wrap and divide the chicken between the wraps, roll

like a burrito, tucking the sides in to hold to secure the ingredients in. Cut in halves and server.

PER SERVING

Cal479, total fat 17 g, chol67 mg, sodium 653 mg, carb49 g, fiber5 g, protein15 g

Mexican Style Burritos

Prep time: 10 minutes | Cook time: 15 minutes| Serves 2

- 1 tablespoon olive oil
- 2 corn tortillas
- ¼ cup red onion chopped
- ¼ cup red bell peppers, chopped
- ½ red chili, deseeded and chopped
- 2 eggs
- juice of 1 lime
- 1 tablespoon cilantro,chopped

1. Turn the broiler to medium heat and place the tortillas underneath for 1 to 2 minutes on each side or until lightly toasted.
2. Remove and keep the broiler on.
3. Sauté onion, chili and bell peppers for 5 to 6 minutes or until soft.
4. Place the eggs on top of the onions and peppers and place skillet under the broiler for 5-6 minutes or until the eggs are cooked.
5. Serve half the eggs and vegetables on top of each tortilla and sprinkle with cilantro and lime juice to serve

PER SERVING

Calories: 202 ,Fat: 13g ,Carb: 19g ,Phosphorus: 184mg ,Potassium: 233mg ,Sodium: 77mg ,Protein: 9g

Keto Egg Fast Snickerdoodle Crepes

Prep time: 10 minutes | Cook time: 15 minutes| Serves 2

- 5 oz cream cheese, softened
- 6 eggs
- 1 teaspoon cinnamon
- Butter, for frying
- 1 tablespoon Swerve
- 2 tablespoons granulated Swerve
- 8 tablespoons butter, softened
- 1 tablespoon cinnamon

1. For the crepes: Put all the ingredients together in a blender except the butter and process until smooth.
2. Heat butter on medium heat in a non-stick pan and pour some batter in the pan.
3. Cook for about 2 minutes, then flip and cook for 2 more minutes.
4. Repeat with the remaining mixture.
5. Mix Swerve, butter and cinnamon in a small bowl until combined.
6. Spread this mixture onto the centre of the crepe and serve rolled up.

PER SERVING

Calories: 543 Carbs: 8g Fats: 51.6g Proteins: 15.7g Sodium: 455mg Sugar: 0.9g

Olive Frittata

Prep time: 10 minutes | Cook time: 15 minutes| Serves 5

- 9 large eggs, lightly beaten
- 8 kalamata olives, pitted, chopped
- 1/4 cup olive oil
- 1/3 cup parmesan cheese, freshly grated
- 1/3 cup fresh basil, thinly sliced
- 1/2 teaspoon salt
- 1/2 teaspoon pepper
- 1/2 cup onion, chopped
- 1 sweet red pepper, diced
- 1 medium zucchini, cut to 1/2-inch cubes
- 1 package (4 ounce) feta cheese, crumbled

1. In a 10-inch oven-proof skillet, heat the olive oil until hot. Add the olives, zucchini, red pepper, and the onions, constantly stirring, until the vegetables are tender.
2. Ina bowl, mix the eggs, feta cheese, basil, salt, and pepper; pour in the skillet with vegetables. Adjust heat to medium-low, cover, and cook for about 10-12 minutes, or until the egg mixture is almost set.
3. Remove from the heat and sprinkle with the parmesan cheese. Transfer to the broiler.
4. With oven door partially open, broil 5 1/2 from the source of heat for about 2-3 minutes or until the top is golden. Cut into wedges.

PER SERVING

Cal288.5, total fat 22.8 g, chol301 mg, sodium 656 mg, carb 5.6 g, fiber1.2 g, sugar3.3g, protein15.2 g.

Chilled Green Goddess Soup

Prep time: 10 minutes | Cook time: 10 minutes| Serves 3

- 6 cups cucumber
- 2 stalks celery chopped
- 1-2 cups water (depending how thin you want it)
- 2 tablespoons fresh lime juice
- 1 cup watercress leaves
- 1 cup rocket leaves
- ½ cup mashed avocado (roughly 1 avocado)
- 1 teaspoon wheatgrass power or a mixed green powder, optional
- Sea salt to tast

1. Blend all ingredients except the avocado in a blender until a broth forms. Strain the liquid through a cheesecloth or fine sieve. Then return to blender and add the avocado and blend until smooth.
2. Garnish with a few watercress leaves and cracked black pepper.

PER SERVING

Calories 283.6, fat 11.5g , carbs31g , protein 10.9g

Detox Porridge

Prep time: 10 minutes | Cook time: 5 minutes| Serves 2

- 1 cup unsweetened almond milk
- 2 tablespoons ground golden flax
- 1/2 cup coconut flour
- 1 tablespoon coconut oil
- 1 teaspoon cinnamon
- 1 cup water
- 1 tablespoon raw honey
- Toasted coconut to serve
- Toasted almonds to serve

1. In a microwave safe bowl, stir together all the ingredients until well combined; place in the microwave and heat for 1 minute.
2. Stir again to mix well and microwave for another 1 minute. Serve right away topped with toasted almonds and toasted coconut.

PER SERVING

Calories242, Carbs 7g , Fat 19g , Protein 12g

Sweet Cream Cheese Breakfast

Prep time: 10 minutes | Cook time: 30 minutes| Serves 3

- 400 g of grainy cream cheese
- 120 g strawberries
- 100 g blueberries
- 1 tbsp lemon juice
- Fresh mint

1. Wash and clean the strawberries and cut into small pieces. Wash blueberries.
2. Pour the cream cheese into a bowl and mix with the berries and lemon juice.
3. Wash the mint, shake dry and pluck some leaves.
4. Fill the cream cheese into two bowls, garnish with a few mint leaves and serve.

PER SERVING

Calories: 300, Total Fat17g, ,Cholesterol 16mg, Sodium59mg ,Total Carbohydrates 34g, Fiber 2g ,Protein: 7g

Beets Omelette

Prep time: 10 minutes | Cook time: 10 minutes| Serves 1

- 2 eggs
- ¼ tsp salt
- ¼ tsp black pepper
- 1 tablespoon olive oil
- ¼ cup cheese
- ¼ tsp basil
- 1 cup beets

1. In a bowl combine all ingredients together and mix well.
2. In a skillet heat olive oil and pour the egg mixture.
3. Cook for 1-2 minutes per side.
4. When ready remove omelette from the skillet and serve.

PER SERVING

Carbs50g, fat 11g, protein 10g, Calories 320

Chapter 5
Drinks Recipes and Smoothie Recipes

Fats Burning & Water Based Smoothies

Prep time: 10 minutes | **Cook time:** 10 minutes| **Serves 2**

- 4 big strawberries
- 1 small piece of banana or an apple slice with peel
- ¼ teaspoon of cinnamon powder
- 1 teaspoon honey

1. Take a blender and add water, remove stems from the berries and add in the blender, put cinnamon powder, honey, crushed ice cubes and remaining fruit. Mix and serve.

PER SERVING

Calories 170, Fat 3, Fiber 6, Carbs 8, Protein 5

Papaya Juice

Prep time: 10 minutes | **Cook time:** 10 minutes| **Serves 2**

- ½ cup papaya cubes
- ½ cup coconut
- ½ cup coconut water
- 1 cup ice

1. In a blender place all ingredients and blend until smooth.
2. Pour smoothie in a glass and serve.

PER SERVING

Calories 191, Fat 10, Fiber 3, Carbs 13, Protein 1

Watermelon Drink

Prep time: 10 minutes | **Cook time:** 10 minutes| **Serves 2**

- 2 cups watermelon
- ¼ cup tomatoes
- ¼ cup apples
- ¼ cup pears

1. In a blender place all ingredients and blend until smooth.
2. Pour smoothie in a glass and serve.

PER SERVING

Calories 140, Fat 4, Fiber 2, Carbs 7, Protein 8

Blue Breeze Shake

Prep time: 10 minutes | **Cook time:** 10 minutes| **Serves 2**

- ½ cup blueberries
- 1 small banana
- 1 cup chilled unsweetened vanilla almond milk
- Water as needed
- 1 scoop unflavored protein powder

1. Mix in a blender for 40-50 seconds and serve as ready.

PER SERVING

Calories 476, Fat 40, Fiber 9, Carbs 33, Protein 6

Glory Smoothie

Prep time: 10 minutes | **Cook time:** 10 minutes| **Serves 2**

- ¼ cup kale
- A handful of romaine
- A handful of broccoli stems
- A celery stalk
- 1cup juice of green apple
- 2 big cucumber slices
- ½ of a lemon juice and zest both

1. This smoothie is preparation ared by combining all ingredients listed above with juice and shake well to form a smooth drink to serve.
2. Use ice or chilled juice to get drink chilled.

PER SERVING

Calories 69, Fat 6.5 g, Fiber 2.6 g, Carbs 10.6 g, Protein 9.4 g

Beetroot & Parsley Smoothie

Prep time: 10 minutes | **Cook time:** 10 minutes| **Serves 2**

- 1 cup carrot
- 1 cup beetroot
- 1 tablespoon parsley
- 1 tablespoon celery
- 1 cup ice

1. In a blender place all ingredients and blend until smooth.
2. Pour smoothie in a glass and serve.

PER SERVING

Calories 100, Fat 1, Fiber 2, Carbs 2, Protein 6

Red Capsicum Juice

Prep time: 10 minutes | **Cook time:** 10 minutes| **Serves 2**

- 1 cup red capsicum
- 1 cup carrot
- 1 cup apple
- 1 cup ice

1. In a blender place all ingredients and blend until smooth.
2. Pour smoothie in a glass and serve.

PER SERVING

Calories 69, Fat 6.5 g, Fiber 2.6 g, Carbs 10.6 g, Protein 9.4 g

Soothing Smoothie for Stomach
Prep time: 10 minutes | Cook time: 10 minutes| Serves 2

- 1 teaspoon brown sugar
- 1 teaspoon lime juice
- 1 cup lite coconut milk
- ¾ cup papaya

1. Pour a cup of the milk in an electric blender and mix in the lime juice, papaya and sugar then mix and serve, add ice if you want to in crushed form only 2-3 cubes.

PER SERVING

Calories 191, Fat 10, Fiber 3, Carbs 13, Protein 1

Lemon and Garlic Smoothie
Prep time: 10 minutes | Cook time: 10 minutes| Serves 2

- 1 lemon juice
- 1 small clove of fresh garlic
- 1 glass water
- Few mint leaves
- 1 teaspoon brown sugar

1. Chop, slice or crush garlic clove and add in an electric mixer with water, lemon juice, sugar and mint leaves to blend and serve immediately. It is better to serve warm.

PER SERVING

Calories 170, Fat 3, Fiber 6, Carbs 8, Protein 5

Smooth Root Green Cleansing Smoothie
Prep time: 10 minutes | Cook time: 10 minutes| Serves 2

- ½ cup fresh lettuce leaves
- ¼ green apple chunks
- A handful of cilantro
- ¼ lime juice
- Couple of cucumber slices
- 1 date without pit
- 1 cup chilled water

1. Wash apple and leaves well before use, do not peel apple just remove seeds and inedible parts, mix all the ingredients blend and serve.

PER SERVING

Calories 140, Fat 4, Fiber 2, Carbs 7, Protein 8

Strawberry Nutty Smoothie
Prep time: 10 minutes | Cook time: 10 minutes| Serves 2

- ½ cup strawberries
- 1 cup nut milk
- 1 tablespoon honey
- 2 slices of orange
- 2 drops of lemon juice
- ½ of a banana slices
- ¼ cup spinach

1. You can also use any skimmed milk, remove stems of strawberries and after washing all foods, chop and mix them in a blender to shake and serve in a glass.

PER SERVING

Calories 69, Fat 6.5 g, Fiber 2.6 g, Carbs 10.6 g, Protein 9.4 g

Power Detox Smoothie
Prep time: 10 minutes | Cook time: 10 minutes| Serves 2

- 1 tablespoon honey
- 1 cup almond milk (unsweetened)
- 1 teaspoon ginger paste
- A pinch of flaxseeds
- ¼ cup cherries without pits
- Ice to chill
- Few drops lemon juice

1. Blend milk with cherries first and then add the rest of the ingredients with ice. Serve chilled.

PER SERVING

Calories 69, Fat 6.5 g, Fiber 2.6 g, Carbs 10.6 g, Protein 9.4 g

Twin Berry Smoothie
Prep time: 10 minutes | Cook time: 10 minutes| Serves 2

- ½ cup peach chunks
- ¾ cup almond milk
- A handful of cranberries and raspberries
- Peel of an orange
- 1 scoop protein powder (whey)
- Ice cubes as required

1. Chop berries well, use natural orange peel, add all foods in a blender and shake to serve.

PER SERVING

Calories 150, Fat 3, Fiber 2, Carbs 6, Protein 8

Cashew Boost Smoothie
Prep time: 10 minutes | **Cook time:** 10 minutes| **Serves 2**

- 2/4 cup raw cashews
- 1 cup chilled almond milk
- ¼ cup mixed fruit

1. Grind all ingredients mixed and serve.

PER SERVING

Calories 191, Fat 10, Fiber 3, Carbs 13, Protein 1

Carrot Drink
Prep time: 10 minutes | **Cook time:** 10 minutes| **Serves 2**

- 2 cups carrots
- 1 cup apple
- ½ tsp brown sugar

1. In a blender place all ingredients and blend until smooth.
2. Pour smoothie in a glass and serve.

PER SERVING

Calories 140, Fat 4, Fiber 2, Carbs 7, Protein 8

Kale Batch Detox Smoothie
Prep time: 10 minutes | **Cook time:** 10 minutes| **Serves 2**

- ¼ cup kale
- 1 cup chilled coconut water
- 2 pear slices
- ¼ cup avocado
- A handful of cilantro

1. Blend all the ingredients in a blender for a minute and serve fresh.

PER SERVING

Calories 191, Fat 10, Fiber 3, Carbs 13, Protein 1

Oatmeal Blast With Fruit
Prep time: 10 minutes | **Cook time:** 10 minutes| **Serves 2**

- ½ cup oats (steel cut)
- A pinch of ground cinnamon
- Ice cubes as needed
- 1 cup water
- ½ cup pineapple chunks

1. Throw oats in a blender and slightly blend with water, add the fruit and other ingredients afterwards and blend again

PER SERVING

Calories 150, Fat 3, Fiber 2, Carbs 6, Protein 8

White Bean Smoothie to Burn Fats
Prep time: 10 minutes | **Cook time:** 10 minutes| **Serves 2**

- 1 cup unsweetened rice milk (chilled)
- ¼ cup peach slices
- ¼ cup white beans cooked
- A pinch of cinnamon powder
- A pinch of nutmeg

1. Pour milk in the blender and add other ingredients to blend till smooth enough to serve and drink.

PER SERVING

Calories 150, Fat 3, Fiber 2, Carbs 6, Protein 8

Muskmelon Juice
Prep time: 10 minutes | **Cook time:** 10 minutes| **Serves 2**

- 2 cups muskmelon
- 2 cups pineapple
- 1 cup ice

1. In a blender place all ingredients and blend until smooth.
2. Pour smoothie in a glass and serve.

PER SERVING

Calories 191, Fat 10, Fiber 3, Carbs 13, Protein 1

Green Tea Purifying Smoothie
Prep time: 10 minutes | **Cook time:** 10 minutes| **Serves 2**

- 2 C. fresh baby spinach
- 3 C. frozen green grapes
- 1 medium ripe avocado peeled, pitted and chopped
- 2 tsp. organic honey
- 1½ C. strong brewed green tea

1. a high-speed blender, add all ingredients and pulse until smooth.
2. Transfer into serving glasses and serve immediately.

PER SERVING

Calories 476, Fat 40, Fiber 9, Carbs 33, Protein 6

Chapter 6
Lunch

Artichoke Feta Penne

Prep time: 10 minutes | Cook time: 30 minutes| Serves 4

- 8 oz. penne pasta
- 2 tablespoons olive oil
- 1 shallot, chopped
- 4 garlic cloves, chopped
- 1 jar artichoke hearts, drained and chopped
- 1 cup diced tomatoes
- ¼ cup white wine
- ½ cup vegetable stock
- Salt and pepper to taste
- 4 oz. feta cheese, crumbled

1. Heat the oil in a skillet and stir in the shallot and garlic. Cook for 2 minutes until softened.
2. Add the artichoke hearts, tomatoes, wine and stock, as well as salt and pepper to taste.
3. Cook on low heat for 15 minutes.
4. In the meantime, cook the penne in a large pot of water until al dente, not more than 8 minutes.
5. Drain the pasta well and mix it with the artichoke sauce.
6. Serve the penne with crumbled feta cheese.

PER SERVING

Calories:325, Fat14.4g, Protein11.1g,
Carbohydrates35.8g

Quinoa & Black Bean Stuffed Sweet Potatoes

Prep time: 10 minutes | Cook time: 60 minutes| Serves 8

- 4 sweet potatoes
- ½ onion, diced
- 1 garlic glove, crushed and diced
- ½ large bell pepper diced (about 2/3 cups)
- Handful of diced cilantro
- ½ cup cooked quinoa
- ½ cup black beans
- 1 tbsp olive oil
- 1 tbsp chili powder
- ½ tbsp cumin
- ½ tbsp paprika
- ½ tbsp oregano
- 2 tbsp lime juice
- 2 tbsp honey
- Sprinkle salt
- 1 cup shredded cheddar cheese
- Chopped spring onions, for garnish (optional)

1. Preheat oven to 400oF.
2. Wash and scrub outside of potatoes. Poke with fork a few times and then place on parchment paper on cookie sheet. Bake for 40-45 minutes or until it is cooked.
3. While potatoes are baking, sauté onions, garlic, olive oil and spices in a pan on the stove until onions are translucent and soft.
4. In the last 10 minutes while the potatoes are cooking, in a large bowl combine the onion mixture with the beans, quinoa, honey, lime juice, cilantro and ½ cup cheese. Mix well.
5. When potatoes are cooked, remove from oven and let cool slightly. When cool to touch, cut in half (hot dog style) and scoop out most of the insides. Leave a thin ring of potato so that it will hold its shape. You can save the sweet potato guts for another recipe, such as my veggie burgers (recipe posted below).
6. Fill with bean and quinoa mixture. Top with remaining cheddar cheese.
7. (If making this a freezer meal, stop here. Individually wrap potato skins in plastic wrap and place on flat surface to freeze. Once frozen, place all potatoes in large zip lock container or Tupperware.)
8. Return to oven for an additional 10 minutes or until cheese is melted.

PER SERVING

Calories 243, Carbs 37.6g, Protein 8.5g, Fat: 7.3g

Smoked Salmon and Watercress Salad

Prep time: 10 minutes | Cook time: 10 minutes| Serves 4

- 2 bunches watercress
- 1 pound smoked salmon, skinless, boneless and flaked
- 2 teaspoons mustard
- ¼ cup lemon juice
- ½ cup Greek yogurt
- Salt and black pepper to the taste
- 1 big cucumber, sliced
- 2 tablespoons chives, chopped

1. In a salad bowl, combine the salmon with the watercress and the rest of the ingredients toss and serve right away.

PER SERVING
Calories 244,Fat 16.7 g ,Fiber 4.5 g,Carbs 22.5 g,Protein 15.6 g

Halloumi, Grape Tomato And Zucchini Skewers

Prep time: 10 minutes | Cook time: 10 minutes| Serves 3

- 1 large zucchini, halved lengthways, cut into 8 pieces
- 16 grape tomatoes
- 180 g halloumi cheese, cut into 16 pieces
- Olive oil spray
- For the spinach-basil oil:
- 2 cups baby spinach leaves
- 2 cups fresh basil leaves
- 185 ml (3/4 cup) extra-virgin olive oil
- 125 ml (1/2 cup) light olive oil

1. In a saucepan of boiling water, cook the spinach and the basil for about 30 seconds or until just wilted. Drain and cool under running cold water.
2. Place the cooked spinach and basil into a food processor. Add the light olive oil and the extra-virgin olive oil; process until the mixture is smooth. Transfer into an airtight container, refrigerate for 8 hours to develop the flavors.
3. Preheat the barbecue grill to medium-high.
4. Thread a piece of zucchini, halloumi cheese, and tomato into each skewer. Lightly spray with the olive oil spray.
5. Grill for about4 minutes per side or until cooked through and golden brown.
6. Arrange the grilled skewers on to serving platter; serve immediately with the preparation ared spinach-basil oil.

PER SERVING
Cal192.2, total fat 20 g, carb1 g, fiber1 g, sugar1 g,protein 3 g, sodium 328.8 mg

Cajun Garlic Shrimp Noodle Bowl

Prep time: 10 minutes | Cook time:15 minutes| Serves 2

- ½ teaspoon salt
- 1 onion, sliced
- 1 red pepper, sliced
- 1 tablespoon butter
- 1 teaspoon garlic granules
- 1 teaspoon onion powder
- 1 teaspoon paprika
- 2 large zucchinis, cut into noodle strips
- 20 jumbo shrimps, shells removed and deveined
- 3 cloves garlic, minced
- 3 tablespoon ghee
- A dash of cayenne pepper
- A dash of red pepper flake

1. Preparation are the Cajun seasoning by mixing the onion powder, garlic granules, pepper flakes, cayenne pepper, paprika and salt. Toss in the shrimp to coat in the seasoning.
2. In a skillet, heat the ghee and sauté the garlic. Add in the red pepper and onions and continue sautéing for 4 minutes.
3. Add the Cajun shrimp and cook until opaque. Set aside.
4. In another pan, heat the butter and sauté the zucchini noodles for three minutes.
5. Assemble by the placing the Cajun shrimps on top of the zucchini noodles.

PER SERVING

Calories: 712 ,Fat: 30.0g ,Protein: 97.8g ,Carbs: 20.2g

Kidney Bean and Parsley-lemon Salad

Prep time: 10 minutes | Cook time: 10 minutes| Serves 6

- ¼ cup lemon juice (about 1 ½ lemons)
- ¼ cup olive oil
- ¾ cup chopped fresh parsley
- ¾ teaspoon salt
- 1 can (15 ounces) chickpeas, rinsed and drained, or 1 ½ cups cooked chickpeas
- 1 medium cucumber, peeled, seeded and diced
- 1 small red onion, diced
- 2 cans (15 ounces each) red kidney beans, rinsed and drained, or 3 cups cooked kidney beans
- 2 stalks celery, sliced in half or thirds lengthwise and chopped
- 2 tablespoons chopped fresh dill or mint
- 3 cloves garlic, pressed or minced
- Small pinch red pepper flakes

1. Whisk well in a small bowl the pepper flakes, salt, garlic, and lemon juice until emulsified.
2. In a serving bowl, combine the preparation ared kidney beans, chickpeas, onion, celery, cucumber, parsley and dill (or mint).
3. Drizzle salad with the dressing and toss well to coat.
4. Serve and enjoy.

PER SERVING

Calories per serving: 228; Protein: 8.5g; Carbs: 26.2g; Fat: 11.0g

Chicken with Potatoes Olives & Sprouts

Prep time: 10 minutes | Cook time: 35 minutes | Serves 4

- 1 lb. chicken breasts, skinless, boneless, and cut into pieces
- ¼ cup olives, quartered
- 1 tsp oregano
- 1½ tsp Dijon mustard
- 1 lemon juice
- 1/3 cup vinaigrette dressing
- 1 medium onion, diced
- 3 cups potatoes cut into pieces
- 4 cups Brussels sprouts, trimmed and quartered
- ¼ tsp pepper
- ¼ tsp salt

1. Warm-up oven to 400 F. Place chicken in the center of the baking tray, then place potatoes, sprouts, and onions around the chicken.
2. In a small bowl, mix vinaigrette, oregano, mustard, lemon juice, and salt and pour over chicken and veggies. Sprinkle olives and season with pepper.
3. Bake in preheated oven for 20 minutes. Transfer chicken to a plate. Stir the vegetables and roast for 15 minutes more. Serve and enjoy.

PER SERVING

Calories: 397 ,Fat: 13g ,Protein: 38.3g ,Carbs: 31.4g ,Sodium 175 mg

Avocado Boat with Salsa

Prep time: 10 minutes | Cook time: 30 minutes | Serves 2

- 1 medium avocado
- 2 medium-sized eggs
- 1 large tomato
- 1 teaspoon lemon juice
- ½ red onion
- 1 teaspoon olive oil
- 1 tsp white wine vinegar
- Salt and pepper

1. Preheat the oven to 175 degrees top and bottom heat.
2. Halve the avocado lengthways, remove the stone and brush the flesh with the lemon juice.
3. Line a baking sheet with a piece of parchment paper and spread the avocado halves on top. Slide an egg into the hollow of the core and sprinkle with a little salt.
4. Bake on the middle rack for 15-20 minutes.
5. In the meantime, preparation are the salsa. To do this, peel and finely chop the onion and wash the tomato and cut into fine cubes. Mix both together with the olive oil and vinegar in a bowl. Season to taste with salt and pepper.
6. Take the avocado out of the oven and serve with the salsa on two plates.

PER SERVING

Calories: 300, Total Fat 17g , Cholesterol 16mg, Sodium 59mg, Total Carbohydrates34g ,Fiber 2g, Protein 7g

Cream Cheese Artichoke Mix

Prep time: 10 minutes | Cook time: 45 minutes| Serves 6

- 4 sheets matzo
- ½ cup artichoke hearts, canned
- 1 cup cream cheese
- 1 cup spinach, chopped
- ½ teaspoon salt
- 1 teaspoon ground black pepper
- 3 tablespoons fresh dill, chopped
- 3 eggs, beaten
- 1 teaspoon canola oil
- ½ cup cottage cheese

1. In the bowl combine together cream cheese, spinach, salt, ground black pepper, dill, and cottage cheese.
2. Pour canola oil in the skillet, add artichoke hearts and roast them for 2-3 minutes over the medium heat. Stir them from time to time.
3. Then add roasted artichoke hearts in the cheese mixture.
4. Add eggs and stir until homogenous.
5. Place one sheet of matzo in the casserole mold.
6. Then spread it with cheese mixture generously.
7. Cover the cheese layer with the second sheet of matzo.
8. Repeat the steps till you use all ingredients.
9. Then preheat oven to 360F.
10. Bake matzo mina for 40 minutes.
11. Cut the cooked meal into the servings.

PER SERVING

Calories 272, fat 17.3, fiber 4.3, carbs 20.2, protein 11.8

Low Carb Berry Salad with Citrus Dressing

Prep time: 10 minutes | Cook time: 10 minutes| Serves 3

- Salad:
- ¼ cup blueberries
- ½ cup chopped strawberries
- 1 cup mixed greens (kale and chard)
- 2 cups baby spinach
- 2 chopped green onions
- ½ cup chopped avocado
- 1 shredded carrots
- Citrus Dressing:
- 1 tablespoon extra-virgin olive oil
- 2 tablespoons apple cider vinegar
- ¼ cup fresh orange juice
- 5 strawberries chopped

1. In a blender, blend together all dressing ingredients until very smooth; set aside.
2. Combine all salad ingredients in a large bowl; drizzle with dressing and toss to coat well before serving.

PER SERVING

Calories 300, Total Fat17g,Fat4g, Cholesterol16mg, Sodium 59mg, Total Carbohydrates 34g, Fiber 2g, Protein 7g

Leek, Bacon and Pea Risotto

Prep time: 10 minutes | Cook time: 60 minutes| Serves 4

- Salt and pepper to taste
- 2 tbsp fresh lemon juice
- ½ cup grated parmesan cheese
- ¾ cup frozen peas
- 1 cup dry white wine
- 2 ½ cups Arborio rice
- 4 slices bacon (cut into strips)
- 12 cups low sodium chicken broth
- 2 leeks cut lengthwise

1. In a saucepan, bring the broth to a simmer over medium flame.
2. On another skillet, cook bacon and stir continuously to avoid the bacon from burning. Cook more for five minutes and add the leeks and cook for two more minutes.
3. Increase the heat to medium high and add the rice until the grains become translucent.
4. Add the wine and stir until it evaporates.
5. Add 1 cup of broth to the mixture and reduce the heat to medium low. Stir constantly for two minutes.
6. Gradually add the remaining broth until the rice becomes al dente and it becomes creamy.
7. Add the peas and the rest of the broth.
8. Remove the skillet or turn off the heat and add the Parmesan cheese.
9. Cover the skillet and let the cheese melt. Season the risotto with lemon juice, salt and pepper.
10. Serve the risotto with more parmesan cheese.

PER SERVING

Calories 742, Carbs 57.6g, Protein 38.67g, Fat39.6g

Zucchini and Mozzarella Casserole

Prep time: 10 minutes | Cook time: 30 minutes| Serves 2

- 400 g ground poultry
- 125 g mozzarella
- 2 medium zucchini
- 1 medium onion
- 1 clove of garlic
- 1 tbsp tomato paste
- 100 ml vegetable broth
- 2 teaspoons of olive oil
- ½ teaspoon dried thyme
- ½ teaspoon dried oregano
- ½ teaspoon dried basil
- Salt and pepper

1. Preheat the oven to 150 degrees top and bottom heat.
2. Wash the zucchini and cut into thin slices.
3. Grease a baking dish with 1 teaspoon of olive oil and arrange some of the zucchini slices evenly in the dish.
4. Peel onions and cut them into fine pieces. Heat the remaining olive oil in a pan and fry the onion, garlic and minced meat in it until the minced meat has a crumbly consistency. Then stir in the tomato paste and season with a little salt and pepper and season with thyme, oregano and basil.
5. Spread part of the minced meat mixture over the zucchini slices. Put another zucchini slices on top and distribute the remaining minced meat mixture on top.
6. Drain the mozzarella, cut into slices and spread on the casserole.
7. Bake on the middle rack for 20-25 minutes.
8. Take out of the oven, let cool down a little and serve.

PER SERVING

Calories 300, Total Fat 17g, Cholesterol16mg, Sodium 59mg, Total Carbohydrates 34g, Fiber 2g, Protein 7g

Meat Cakes

Prep time: 10 minutes | Cook time: 10 minutes| Serves 4

- 1 cup broccoli, shredded
- ½ cup ground pork
- 2 eggs, beaten
- 1 teaspoon salt
- 1 tablespoon Italian seasonings
- 1 teaspoon olive oil
- 3 tablespoons wheat flour, whole grain
- 1 tablespoon dried dill

1. In the mixing bowl combine together shredded broccoli and ground pork,
2. Add salt, Italian seasoning, flour, and dried dill.
3. Mix up the mixture until homogenous.
4. Then add eggs and stir until smooth.
5. Heat up olive oil in the skillet.
6. With the help of the spoon make latkes and place them in the hot oil.
7. Roast the latkes for 4 minutes from each side over the medium heat.
8. The cooked latkes should have a light brown crust.
9. Dry the latkes with the paper towels if needed.

PER SERVING

Calories 143, fat 6, fiber 0.9, carbs 7, protein 15.1

Grilled Basil-lemon Tofu Burgers

Prep time: 10 minutes | Cook time: 10 minutes| Serves 5

- 6 slices (1/4-inch thick each) tomato
- 6 pieces (1 1/2-ounce) whole-wheat hamburger buns
- 1 pound tofu, firm or extra-firm, drained
- 1 cup watercress, trimmed
- Cooking spray
- 1/3 cup fresh basil, finely chopped
- 2 tablespoons Dijon mustard
- 2 tablespoons honey
- 1/4 cup freshly squeezed lemon juice
- 2 teaspoons grated lemon rind
- 1 tablespoon olive oil, extra-virgin,
- 1/2 teaspoon salt
- 1/4 teaspoon black pepper (freshly ground)
- 3 garlic cloves, minced
- 1 garlic cloves, minced
- 1/3 cup Kalamata olives, finely, chopped pitted
- 3 tablespoons sour cream, reduced-fat
- 3 tablespoons light mayonnai

1. Combine the marinade ingredients in a small-sized bowl. In a crosswise direction, cut the tofu into 6 slices. Pat each piece dry using paper towels. Place them in a jelly roll pan and brush both sides of the slices with the marinade mixture; reserve any leftover marinade. Marinate for 1 hour.
2. Preheat the grill and coated the grill rack with cooking spray. Place the tofu slices; grill for about 3 minutes per side, brushing the tofu with the reserved marinade mixture.
3. In a small-sized bowl, combine the garlic-olive mayonnaise ingredients. Spread about 1 1/2 tablespoons of the mixture over the bottom half of the hamburger buns. Top each with 1 slice tofu, 1 slice tomato, about 2 tablespoons of watercress, and top with the top buns.

PER SERVING

Cal276,total fat 11.3 g, protein 10.5 g, carb34.5 g, fiber1.5 g, chol5 mg, iron 2.4 mg, sodium743 mg

Cod and Mushrooms Mix

Prep time: 10 minutes | Cook time: 25 minutes| Serves 4

- 2 cod fillets, boneless
- 4 tablespoons olive oil
- 4 ounces mushrooms, sliced
- Sea salt and black pepper to the taste
- 12 cherry tomatoes, halved
- 8 ounces lettuce leaves, torn
- 1 avocado, pitted, peeled and cubed
- 1 red chili pepper, chopped
- 1 tablespoon cilantro, chopped
- 2 tablespoons balsamic vinegar
- 1 ounce feta cheese, crumbled

1. Put the fish in a roasting pan, brush it with 2 tablespoons oil, sprinkle salt and pepper all over and broil under medium-high heat for 15 minutes. Meanwhile, heat up a pan with the rest of the oil over medium heat, add the mushrooms, stir and sauté for 5 minutes.
2. Add the rest of the ingredients, toss, cook for 5 minutes more and divide between plates.
3. Top with the fish and serve right away.

PER SERVING

Calories 257 ,Fat 10 g ,Fiber 3.1 g ,Carbs 24.3 g ,Protein 19.4 g

Spanish Rice Casserole with Cheesy Beef

Prep time: 10 minutes | Cook time: 32 minutes| Serves 2

- 2 tablespoons chopped green bell pepper
- 1/4 teaspoon Worcestershire sauce
- 1/4 teaspoon ground cumin
- 1/4 cup shredded Cheddar cheese
- 1/4 cup finely chopped onion
- 1/4 cup chile sauce
- 1/3 cup uncooked long grain rice
- 1/2-pound lean ground beef
- 1/2 teaspoon salt
- 1/2 teaspoon brown sugar
- 1/2 pinch ground black pepper
- 1/2 cup water
- 1/2 (14.5 ounce) can canned tomatoes
- 1 tablespoon chopped fresh cilantro

1. Kvocados mit TomPlace a nonstick saucepan on medium fire and brown beef for 10 minutes while crumbling beef. Discard fat.
2. Stir in pepper, Worcestershire sauce, cumin, brown sugar, salt, chile sauce, rice, water, tomatoes, green bell pepper, and onion. Mix well and cook for 10 minutes until blended and a bit tender.
3. Transfer to an ovenproof casserole and press down firmly. Sprinkle cheese on top and cook for 7 minutes at 400oF preheated oven. Broil for 3 minutes until top is lightly browned.
4. Serve and enjoy with chopped cilantro.

PER SERVING

Calories 460, Carbohydrates 35.8g, Protein37.8g, Fat 17.9g

White Bean Soup

Prep time: 10 minutes | Cook time: 8 Hours 30 Minutes | Serves 6

- 1 cup celery, chopped
- 1 cup carrots, chopped
- 1 yellow onion, chopped
- 6 cups veggie stock
- 4 garlic cloves, minced
- 2 cup navy beans, dried
- ½ teaspoon basil, dried
- ½ teaspoon sage, dried
- 1 teaspoon thyme, dried
- A pinch of salt and black pepper

1. In your slow cooker, combine the beans with the stock and the rest of the ingredients, put the lid on and cook on Low for 8 hours.
2. Divide the soup into bowls and serve right away.

PER SERVING

Calories 264, fat 17.5, fiber 4.5, carbs 23.7, protein 11.5

Balsamic Steak with Feta, Tomato, and Basil

Prep time: 10 minutes | Cook time: 20 minutes | Serves 4

- 1 tablespoon balsamic vinegar
- 1/4 cup basil leaves
- 175 g Greek fetta, crumbled
- 2 tablespoons olive oil
- 2 teaspoons baby capers
- 4 sirloin steaks, trimmed
- 4 whole garlic cloves, skin on
- 6 roma tomatoes, halved
- Olive oil spray
- Salt and cracked black pepper

1. Preheat the oven to 200C.
2. Line a baking tray with baking paper. Place the tomatoes and then scatter with the capers, crumbled feta, and the garlic cloves. Drizzle with 1 tablespoon of the olive oil and season with salt and pepper; cook for about 15 minutes or until the tomatoes are soft. Remove from the oven, set aside.
3. In a large non-metallic bowl, toss the steak with the remaining 1 tablespoon of olive oil, vinegar, salt and pepper; cover and refrigerate for 5 minutes.
4. Preheat the grill pan to high heat; grill the steaks for about 4 minutes per side or until cooked to your preference.
5. Serve with the preparation ared tomato mixture and sprinkle with basil.

PER SERVING

Cal520.3, total fat30 g, carb 3 g, fiber2 g, sugar2 g, protein 59 g, sodium 622.82 mg

Roasted Butternut Squash Salad with Warm Cider Vinaigrette

Prep time: 15 minutes | Cook time: 35 minutes | Serves 4

- For roasted butternut squash:
- ¾ pound butternut squash, peeled, deseeded, cut into ½ inch pieces
- ½ tablespoon pure maple syrup
- freshly ground black pepper, to taste
- ¾ teaspoon extra-virgin olive oil
- fine sea salt or Kosher salt, to taste
- ½ tablespoon dried cranberries
- For warm cider vinaigrette dressing:
- 6 tablespoons apple cider vinegar or apple juice
- 1 tablespoon minced shallot
- ½ tablespoon extra-virgin olive oil
- freshly ground pepper, to taste
- For the salad:
- 4 walnut halves, toasted
- 2 ounces baby arugula
- ½ tablespoon freshly grated Parmesan cheese

1. Preheat the oven to 400°F.
2. Combine butternut squash, oil, pepper, salt, and maple syrup in a shallow roasting pan.
3. Place the pan in the oven and set the timer for 20 minutes or until tender. Stir the squash after about 12 minutes of baking.
4. To make dressing: Combine vinegar, shallots, and pepper in a small saucepan.
5. Place the saucepan over medium-high heat. Let it simmer until the sauce boils down to about 2 tablespoons. Remove from heat.
6. Add salt, pepper, and oil and whisk well.
7. To serve: Add squash, arugula, and walnuts into a large bowl and toss well.
8. Pour dressing over the salad. Toss well.
9. Garnish with cheese and serve.

PER SERVING ¼ OF THE RECIPE

Calories: 138,Fat: 6 g,Total carbohydrates: 21 g,Protein: 2 g

Turkey and Quinoa Stuffed Peppers
Prep time: 10 minutes | Cook time:55 minutes| Serves 6

- 3 large red bell peppers
- 2 tsp chopped fresh rosemary
- 2 tbsp chopped fresh parsley
- 3 tbsp chopped pecans, toasted
- ¼ cup extra virgin olive oil
- ½ cup chicken stock
- ½ lb. fully cooked smoked turkey sausage, diced
- ½ tsp salt
- 2 cups water
- 1 cup uncooked quinoa

1. On high fire, place a large saucepan and add salt, water and quinoa. Bring to a boil.
2. Once boiling, reduce fire to a simmer, cover and cook until all water is absorbed around 15 minutes.
3. Uncover quinoa, turn off fire and let it stand for another 5 minutes.
4. Add rosemary, parsley, pecans, olive oil, chicken stock and turkey sausage into pan of quinoa. Mix well.
5. Slice peppers lengthwise in half and discard membranes and seeds. In another boiling pot of water, add peppers, boil for 5 minutes, drain and discard water.
6. Grease a 13 x 9 baking dish and preheat oven to 350oF.
7. Place boiled bell pepper onto preparation ared baking dish, evenly fill with the quinoa mixture and pop into oven.
8. Bake for 15 minutes.

PER SERVING

Calories 255.6,Carbs21.6g, Protein 14.4g, Fat: 12.4g

California Poke Bowl
Prep time: 10 minutes| Cook time: 10 minutes| Serves 2

- ¼ cup rice vinegar, divided
- ½ teaspoon black sesame seeds
- 1 tablespoon low-sodium tamari or soy sauce
- ½ teaspoon honey
- ¼ English cucumber, peeled into ribbons
- 2 green onions, thinly sliced on the bias
- ½ jalapeño pepper, deseeded, thinly sliced
- 3 teaspoons sesame oil, divided
- 6 ounces sushi or sashimi grade salmon, cut into ¾ inch chunks
- ½ tablespoon finely grated ginger
- 1 ¼ cups cooked long grain brown rice
- 1 carrot, peeled, cut into matchsticks
- 1 small avocado, peeled, pitted, thinly sliced

1. To make marinade: Add 1 ½ tablespoons of vinegar, sesame seeds, and 1 teaspoon of sesame oil into a bowl and mix well.
2. Add salmon and mix well. Chill until use.
3. To make dressing: Add 2 ½ tablespoons of vinegar, 2 teaspoons sesame oil, ginger, tamari, and honey into another bowl and whisk well.
4. To arrange the bowls: Place rice in a bowl. Pour about half the dressing over the rice and mix well.
5. Distribute the rice into two bowls. Divide equally the cucumber, onion, carrots, jalapeños, and avocado among the bowls.
6. Pour remaining dressing over the vegetables. Distribute equally the marinated salmon among the bowls and serve.

PER SERVING 1 BOWL

Calories: 590,Fat: 33 g,Total carbohydrates: 49 g,Protein: 25 g

Chicken Gyro Bowls

Prep time: 30 minutes| Cook time: 30 minutes| Serves 2

- For the pickles:
- 2 tablespoons water
- 1 teaspoon sugar
- 2 tablespoons cider vinegar
- ¼ cup thinly sliced red onion
- For the sauce:
- ¾ tablespoon tahini
- 1 tablespoon water
- ¼ cup 2% reduced-fat Greek yogurt
- ½ tablespoon fresh lemon juice
- For the bowls:
- 1 cup cooked quinoa
- ½ cup chopped baby kale
- ½ teaspoon onion powder
- ½ teaspoon dried oregano
- ¼ teaspoon Kosher salt, or to taste
- 1 chicken breast cutlet (4 ounces)
- ½ cup halved grape tomatoes
- ¼ cup canned or cooked chickpeas, rinsed, drained
- ¾ ounce feta cheese, crumbled
- 1 teaspoon olive oil, divided
- ⅓ cup chopped fresh flat-leaf parsley
- ½ teaspoon garlic powder
- ¼ teaspoon ground cumin
- pepper, to taste
- ¼ whole-wheat pita (from a 6 inch pita), cut into 3 wedges, separated
- ½ cup thinly sliced cucumber
- 6 kalamata olives, thinly sliced

1. To make the pickles: Add sugar, vinegar, and water into a small microwave safe bowl. Bring to a boil in the microwave on 'High', about a minute or so.
2. Take out the bowl from the microwave. Add onion and stir. Let it rest for 20 minutes. Drain off the liquid from the onion.
3. To make sauce: Add tahini, yogurt, water, and lemon juice into a bowl and mix well. Chill until use.
4. Add quinoa and ½ teaspoon of oil into a bowl. Mix well. Stir in kale and ¼ cup parsley. Cover and set aside until you need to assemble it.
5. Add garlic powder, cumin, pepper, onion powder, oregano, and salt into a bowl and mix well.
6. Pour remaining oil into a skillet and let it heat over medium-high heat.
7. Sprinkle the spice mixture all over the chicken. Press the mixture lightly to adhere.
8. Place the chicken in the pan. Cook until the underside is golden brown. Turn the chicken over and cook the other side until golden brown and cooked through inside.
9. Remove chicken from the pan and place on your cutting board. Let it cool for about 5 minutes. Cut into thin slices.
10. Set up the oven to broil mode and preheat the oven to high heat.
11. Separate the pita wedges. You will get six wedges in all after separating.
12. Place them on a baking sheet, without overlapping. Spray the pita with cooking spray.
13. Place the baking sheet in the oven and broil for 2 minutes or until crisp. Flip sides after a minute of broiling.
14. To assemble the bowls: Divide the quinoa among four bowls. Divide the tomatoes, chickpeas, cheese, chicken, cucumber, olives, and pickled onion among the bowls and place it in whatever manner you prefer.
15. Divide the sauce mixture equally and pour on top. Place three pita wedges on top of each bowl.
16. Garnish with remaining parsley and serve.

PER SERVING 1 BOWL

Calories: 381,Fat: 13.3 g,Total carbohydrates: 41 g,Protein: 26 g

Fish Taco Cabbage Bowls

Prep time: 15 minutes| Cook time: 30 minutes| Serves 2

- 2 small white fish filets
- 1 teaspoon Szeged fish rub, or any other fish rub of your choice
- ¼ teaspoon chili powder
- ¼ medium head red cabbage, thinly sliced
- guacamole to serve, (optional, but recommended)
- 2 teaspoons olive oil
- ½ teaspoon ground cumin
- ½ medium head green cabbage, thinly sliced
- ¼ cup thinly sliced green onions, or use more if desired
- For dressing:
- 1 tablespoon fresh lime juice
- salt, to taste (optional)
- ¼ cup mayonnaise
- 1 teaspoon green Tabasco sauce, or to taste

1. If you are using frozen fish, make sure to thaw it in the refrigerator for 8–10 hours.
2. Add chili powder, fish rub, and cumin into a small bowl. Mix well.
3. Dry the fish by patting with paper towels. Rub 1 teaspoon of oil all over the fish. Sprinkle the spice mixture all over the fish and rub it into the fish.
4. Set it aside for 15–20 minutes.
5. To make dressing: Add lime juice, salt, mayonnaise, and Tabasco sauce into a bowl. And whisk well.
6. Pour a teaspoon of oil into a grill pan and let it heat the pan over medium-high heat.
7. When the pan is hot, place fish in the pan and cook for 4 minutes. Turn the fish over and cook the other side for 4 minutes or until the fish flakes easily when pierced with a fork. Turn off the heat and let the fish cool. Shred into smaller pieces.
8. Place half the green onions, green, and red cabbage in a bowl and mix well.
9. Pour some of the dressing over the cabbage mixture and toss well.
10. To assemble: Divide the salad among two serving bowls. Drizzle remaining dressing on top.
11. Garnish with remaining green onions. Serve with a dollop of guacamole if desired.

PER SERVING 1 BOWL

Calories: 354,Fat: 31 g,Total carbohydrates: 7 g,Protein: 12 g

Kale and Quinoa Bowl

Prep time: 20 minutes| Cook time: 30 minutes| Serves 3

- For the bowl:
- 1 cup quinoa
- ¼ cup freshly cooked chickpeas, drained, cooled
- ½ teaspoon sea salt, divided
- ¼ teaspoon ground cumin
- ¼ cucumber, diced
- 1 red bell pepper, thinly sliced
- ½ tablespoon olive oil
- ¼ teaspoon thinly sliced fresh hot pepper
- 1 bunch kale, discard hard stems and ribs, cut into bite size pieces
- For the sauce:
- ⅛ cup grass-fed cow cream
- ¾ tablespoon olive oil
- ½ tablespoon lemon juice
- 3 cloves garlic, peeled, minced
- ⅛ teaspoon lemon juice

1. Cook the quinoa following the instructions given on the package of quinoa.
2. Fluff the cooked grains with a fork. Let it cool.
3. Meanwhile, pour half the oil into a pan and let it heat over medium heat. Add bell peppers and cook until tender. Turn off the heat.
4. Preheat the oven to 425°F.
5. Dry the chickpeas by patting with paper towels. Remove dangling skin if any from the chickpeas.
6. Spread the chickpeas on a baking sheet and place it in the oven for 20 minutes.
7. Transfer the chickpeas into a bowl. Add hot pepper and cumin and mix well.
8. Place kale in a large bowl. Add ¼ teaspoon of salt over the leaves. Massage the leaves with your hands for a couple of minutes until slightly soft.
9. To make garlic sauce: Add garlic into a small food process jar and blend until you get paste.
10. With the blender machine on, pour oil in a thin drizzle until emulsified.
11. Mix in the yogurt and lemon juice. Add remaining salt and some pepper to taste.
12. Divide quinoa into three bowls. Place cooked bell peppers, chickpeas, and cucumber on top.
13. Spoon the garlic sauce on top and serve.

PER SERVING 1 BOWL

Calories: 392,Fat: 14 g,Total carbohydrates: 55 g,Protein: 14 g

Chapter 7
Dinner

Stewed Chicken Greek Style

Prep time: 10 minutes | Cook time: 60 minutes| Serves 9

- ½ cup red wine
- 1 ½ cups chicken stock or more if needed
- 1 cup olive oil
- 1 cup tomato sauce
- 1 pc, 4lbs whole chicken cut into pieces
- 1 pinch dried oregano or to taste
- 10 small shallots, peeled
- 2 bay leaves
- 2 cloves garlic, finely chopped
- 2 tbsp chopped fresh parsley
- 2 tsps butter
- Salt and ground black pepper to tast

1. Bring to a boil a large pot of lightly salted water. Mix in the shallots and let boil uncovered until tender for around three minutes. Then drain the shallots and dip in cold water until no longer warm.
2. In another large pot over medium fire, heat butter and olive oil until bubbling and melted. Then sauté in the chicken and shallots for 15 minutes or until chicken is cooked and shallots are soft and translucent. Then add the chopped garlic and cook for three mins more.
3. Then add bay leaves, oregano, salt and pepper, parsley, tomato sauce and the red wine and let simmer for a minute before adding the chicken stock. Stir before covering and let cook for 50 minutes on medium-low fire or until chicken is tender.

PER SERVING

Calories 644.8,Carbs 8.2g, Protein 62.1g, Fat: 40.4g

Chicken & Veggies With Toasted Walnuts

Prep time: 10 minutes | Cook time: 15 minutes| Serves 3

- 4 (about 250g) chicken tenderloins
- 1 teaspoon extra virgin olive oil
- 1 small zucchini, sliced
- 2 cups drained and rinsed cannellini beans
- 1 cup chopped green beans
- 1/4 cup pitted and halved green olives
- 1 tablespoon fresh lemon juice
- 2 garlic cloves, sliced
- 400g can cherry tomatoes
- 1 teaspoon harissa paste
- 1 teaspoon smoked paprika
- Fresh parsley sprigs
- 1 cup toasted walnuts, chopped

1. In a plastic container, mix together lemon juice, garlic, harissa, and paprika until well combined; add in chicken and shake to coat well. Let sit a few minutes.
2. Heat oil in a skillet and add in the chicken along with the marinade; cook for about 2 minutes per side or until golden browned.
3. Stir in the veggies and simmer for about 10 minutes or until tender. Divide among serving plates and serve topped with fresh parsley and toasted walnuts.

PER SERVING

Calories 200, Fat 6.0g, Total Carbs 32.4g, Sugars 15.3g, Protein 11.7g

Tasty Beef Stew

Prep time: 10 minutes | Cook time: 30 minutes| Serves 3

- 2 1/2 lbs beef roast, cut into chunks
- 1 cup beef broth
- 1/2 cup balsamic vinegar
- 1 tbsp honey
- 1/2 tsp red pepper flakes
- 1 tbsp garlic, minced
- Pepper
- Salt

1. Add all ingredients into the inner pot of instant pot and stir well.
2. Seal pot with lid and cook on high for 30 minutes.
3. Once done, allow to release pressure naturally. Remove lid.
4. Stir well and serve.

PER SERVING

Calories 562, Fat 18.1 g ,Carbohydrates 5.7 g, Sugar 4.6 g, Protein 87.4 g, Cholesterol 253 mg

Chicken and Lemongrass Sauce

Prep time: 10 minutes | Cook time: 20 minutes| Serves 3

- 1 tablespoon dried dill
- 1 teaspoon butter, melted
- ½ teaspoon lemongrass
- ½ teaspoon cayenne pepper
- 1 teaspoon tomato sauce
- 3 tablespoons sour cream
- 1 teaspoon salt
- 10 oz chicken fillet, cubed

1. Make the sauce: in the saucepan whisk together lemongrass, tomato sauce, sour cream, salt, and dried dill.
2. Bring the sauce to boil.
3. Meanwhile, pour melted butter in the skillet.
4. Add cubed chicken fillet and roast it for 5 minutes. Stir it from time to time.
5. Then place the chicken cubes in the hot sauce.
6. Close the lid and cook the meal for 10 minutes over the low heat.

PER SERVING

Calories 166, fat 8.2, fiber 0.2, carbs 1.1, protein 21

Lemony Lamb and Potatoes

Prep time: 10 minutes | Cook time: 30 minutes| Serves 3

- 2 pound lamb meat, cubed
- 2 tablespoons olive oil
- 2 springs rosemary, chopped
- 2 tablespoons parsley, chopped
- 1 tablespoon lemon rind, grated
- 3 garlic cloves, minced
- 2 tablespoons lemon juice
- 2 pounds baby potatoes, scrubbed and halved
- 1 cup veggie stock

1. In a roasting pan, combine the meat with the oil and the rest of the ingredients, introduce in the oven and bake at 400 degrees F for 2 hours and 10 minutes.
2. Divide the mix between plates and serve.

PER SERVING

Calories 302, fat 15.2, fiber 10.6, carbs 23.3, protein 15.2

Yummy Turkey Meatballs

Prep time: 10 minutes | Cook time: 30 minutes| Serves 3

- ¼ yellow onion, finely diced
- 1 14-oz can of artichoke hearts, diced
- 1 lb. ground turkey
- 1 tsp dried parsley
- 1 tsp oil
- 4 tbsp fresh basil, finely chopped
- Pepper and salt to taste

1. Grease a cookie sheet and preheat oven to 350oF.
2. On medium fire, place a nonstick medium saucepan and sauté artichoke hearts and diced onions for 5 minutes or until onions are soft.
3. Remove from fire and let cool.
4. Meanwhile, in a big bowl, mix with hands parsley, basil and ground turkey. Season to taste.
5. Once onion mixture has cooled add into the bowl and mix thoroughly.
6. With an ice cream scooper, scoop ground turkey and form into balls, makes around 6 balls.
7. Place on preparation ped cookie sheet, pop in the oven and bake until cooked through around 15-20 minutes.
8. Remove from pan, serve and enjoy.

PER SERVING

Calories 328, Carbs 11.8g, Protein 33.5g, Fat 16.3g

Lemon-pepper Tuna Bake

Prep time: 10 minutes | Cook time: 35 minutes| Serves 4

- 4 (140g each) tuna fillets
- 1 bunch asparagus, trimmed
- 3 cups baby potatoes, diced
- 250g cherry tomatoes, diced
- 1 tablespoon extra-virgin olive oil
- 2 lemons, plus lemon zest to serve
- 8 sprigs fresh lemon thyme
- 1/4 teaspoon cracked pepper

1. Preheat your oven to 400 degrees and line a greased baking tray with baking paper. On the preparation ared tray, toss together lemon juice, potatoes, half of thyme, lemon wedges and two teaspoons of oil until well coated.
2. Roast for about 15 minutes and then add in tomatoes; continue cooking for another 10 minutes; place the asparagus and tuna over the veggies and drizzle with the remaining oil.
3. Continue roasting for another 8 minutes. serve topped with lemon zest and thyme. Enjoy!

PER SERVING

Calories 250, Fat 15.5g, Total Carbs 11.5g, Sugars 3.7g, Protein19.2g

Sautéed Cauliflower Delight

Prep time: 10 minutes | Cook time: 30 minutes| Serves 3

- 1 head cauliflower, cut into florets
- 1/4 teaspoon red pepper flakes
- 1/4 cup olive oil
- 1 cup cherry tomatoes, halved, or more to taste
- 1 red onion, chopped
- 1 teaspoon natural sweetener as per your taste (raw honey or maple syrup are good options)
- 2 tablespoons raisins
- 1 clove garlic, minced
- 1 teaspoon dried parsley
- 1 tablespoon fresh lemon juice, or to taste (optional)

1. Set your oil on medium heat to get hot.
2. Cook and stir onion until tender (5 to 10 minutes).
3. Add raisins, cauliflower, sweetener and cherry tomatoes; cover and cook until tender (about 5 minutes), stirring occasionally.
4. Add in your red pepper flakes, parsley and garlic. Switch to high heat and sauté until cauliflower is browned (about 2 minutes).
5. Drizzle lemon juice over cauliflower.

PER SERVING

Calories 476, Fat 40, Fiber 9, Carbs 33, Protein 6

Turkey and Chickpeas

Prep time: 10 minutes | Cook time: 10 minutes| Serves 3

- 2 tablespoons avocado oil
- 1 big turkey breast, skinless, boneless and roughly cubed
- Salt and black pepper to the taste
- 1 red onion, chopped
- 15 ounces canned chickpeas, drained and rinsed
- 15 ounces canned tomatoes, chopped
- 1 cup kalamata olives, pitted and halved
- 2 tablespoons lime juice
- 1 teaspoon oregano, dried

1. Heat up a pan with the oil over medium-high heat, add the meat and the onion, brown for 5 minutes and transfer to a slow cooker.
2. Add the rest of the ingredients, put the lid on and cook on High for 5 hours.
3. Divide between plates and serve right away!

PER SERVING

Calories 352, fat 14.4, fiber 11.8, carbs 25.1, protein 26.4

Chicken Breast & Zucchini Linguine

Prep time: 10 minutes | Cook time: 10 minutes| Serves 3

- 450g chicken breast fillets, halved
- 1 tablespoon olive oil
- 2 garlic cloves, crushed
- 3 cups zucchini noodles
- 1/2 cup coconut cream
- 1/3 cup homemade chicken broth
- 1 tablespoon fresh dill leaves
- 2 tablespoons fresh chives, chopped
- 1 cup baby spinach
- ½ cup toasted chopped cashews

1. Coat a pan with oil and set over medium high heat; season chicken with salt and pepper and cook in the pan for about 3 minutes per side or until cooked through; transfer to a plate and keep warm.
2. Add oil to the pan and sauté garlic until fragrant; stir in zucchini noodles and cook for about 2 minutes; stir in coconut cream and chicken broth and simmer for about 2 minutes or until tender.
3. Slice the chicken and add to the zucchini sauce along with chives and dill. Divide among serving bowls and top each with spinach and toasted cashews.
4. Enjoy!

PER SERVING

Calories 200, Fat6.0g, Total Carbs 32.4g, Sugars15.3g, Protein 11.7g

Ginger Chicken Drumsticks

Prep time: 10 minutes | Cook time: 30 minutes| Serves 4

- 4 chicken drumsticks
- 1 apple, grated
- 1 tablespoon curry paste
- 4 tablespoons milk
- 1 teaspoon coconut oil
- 1 teaspoon chili flakes
- ½ teaspoon minced ginger

1. Mix up together grated apple, curry paste, milk, chili flakes, and minced garlic.
2. Put coconut oil in the skillet and melt it.
3. Add apple mixture and stir well.
4. Then add chicken drumsticks and mix up well.
5. Roast the chicken for 2 minutes from each side.
6. Then preheat oven to 360F.
7. Place the skillet with chicken drumsticks in the oven and bake for 25 minutes.

PER SERVING

Calories 150, fat 6.4, fiber 1.4, carbs 9.7, protein 13.5

Chicken and Semolina Meatballs

Prep time: 10 minutes | Cook time: 10 minutes| Serves 3

- 1/3 cup carrot, grated
- 1 onion, diced
- 2 cups ground chicken
- 1 tablespoon semolina
- 1 egg, beaten
- ½ teaspoon salt
- 1 teaspoon dried oregano
- 1 teaspoon dried cilantro
- 1 teaspoon chili flakes
- 1 tablespoon coconut oil

1. In the mixing bowl combine together grated carrot, diced onion, ground chicken, semolina, egg, salt, dried oregano, cilantro, and chili flakes.
2. With the help of scooper make the meatballs.
3. Heat up the coconut oil in the skillet.
4. When it starts to shimmer, put meatballs in it.
5. Cook the meatballs for 5 minutes from each side over the medium-low heat.

PER SERVING

Calories 102, fat 4.9, fiber 0.5, carbs 2.9, protein 11.2

Beef Dish

Prep time: 10 minutes | Cook time: 20 minutes| Serves 3

- 1 lb. skirt steak
- 2 TB. minced garlic
- 1/4 cup fresh lemon juice
- 2 TB. apple cider vinegar
- 3 TB. extra-virgin olive oil
- 1 tsp. salt
- 1/2 tsp. ground black pepper
- 1/4 tsp. ground cinnamon
- 1/4 tsp. ground cardamom
- 1 tsp. seven spices

1. Using a sharp knife, cut skirt steak into thin, 1/4-inch strips. Place strips in a large bowl.
2. Add garlic, lemon juice, apple cider vinegar, extra-virgin olive oil, salt, black pepper, cinnamon, cardamom, and seven spices, and mix well.
3. Place steak in the refrigerator and marinate for at least 20 minutes and up to 24 hours.
4. Preheat a large skillet over medium heat. Add meat and marinade, and cook for 20 minutes or until meat is tender and marinade has evaporated.
5. Serve warm with pita bread and tahini sauce.

PER SERVING

Calories 476, Fat 40, Fiber 9, Carbs 33, Protein 6

Bulgur and Chicken Skillet

Prep time: 10 minutes | Cook time: 40 minutes| Serves 3

- 4 (6-oz.) skinless, boneless chicken breasts
- 1 tablespoon olive oil, divided
- 1 cup thinly sliced red onion
- 1 tablespoon thinly sliced garlic
- 1 cup unsalted chicken stock
- 1 tablespoon coarsely chopped fresh dill
- 1/2 teaspoon freshly ground black pepper, divided
- 1/2 cup uncooked bulgur
- 2 teaspoons chopped fresh or 1/2 tsp. dried oregano
- 4 cups chopped fresh kale (about 2 1/2 oz.)
- 1/2 cup thinly sliced bottled roasted red bell peppers
- 2 ounces feta cheese, crumbled (about 1/2 cup)
- 3/4 teaspoon kosher salt, divided

1. Place a cast iron skillet on medium high fire and heat for 5 minutes. Add oil and heat for 2 minutes.
2. Season chicken with pepper and salt to taste.
3. Brown chicken for 4 minutes per side and transfer to a plate.
4. In same skillet, sauté garlic and onion for 3 minutes. Stir in oregano and bulgur and toast for 2 minutes.
5. Stir in kale and bell pepper, cook for 2 minutes. Pour in stock and season well with pepper and salt.
6. Return chicken to skillet and turn off fire. Pop in a preheated 400oF oven and bake for 15 minutes.
7. Remove form oven, fluff bulgur and turn over chicken. Let it stand for 5 minutes.
8. Serve and enjoy with a sprinkle of feta cheese.

PER SERVING

Calories 369, Carbs 21.0g, Protein 45.0g, Fats: 11.3g

Grilled Chicken With Rainbow Salad Bowl

Prep time: 10 minutes | Cook time: 10 minutes| Serves 3

- 300g grilled skinless chicken, shredded
- 2 cups mixed salad leaves
- 4 radishes, thinly sliced
- 1 cup chopped tomatoes
- 1 cup shredded carrot
- 1 cup podded edamame
- 4 tablespoons almond butter
- 2 tablespoons freshly squeezed lemon juice
- 2 tablespoons freshly squeezed lime juice
- ½ teaspoon sea salt

1. Blanch edamame in boiling water for about 2 minutes and then drain; transfer to a serving bowl and add in salad leaves, radish, tomatoes, carrots and chicken.
2. In a bowl, whisk together fresh lemon juice, lime juice, almond butter, and sea salt until smooth; drizzle over the salad and serve.

PER SERVING

Calories 381, Fat 28.5g, Total Carbs 30.8g, Sugars 17.4g, Protein6.4

Bell Peppers On Chicken Breasts

Prep time: 10 minutes | Cook time: 30 minutes| Serves 6

- ¼ tsp freshly ground black pepper
- ½ tsp salt
- 1 large red bell pepper, cut into ¼-inch strips
- 1 large yellow bell pepper, cut into ¼-inch strips
- 1 tbsp olive oil
- 1 tsp chopped fresh oregano
- 2 1/3 cups coarsely chopped tomato
- 2 tbsp finely chopped fresh flat-leaf parsley
- 20 Kalamata olives
- 3 cups onion sliced crosswise
- 6 4-oz skinless, boneless chicken breast halves, cut in half horizontally
- Cooking spray

1. On medium high fire, place a large nonstick fry pan and heat oil. Once oil is hot, sauté onions until soft and translucent, around 6 to 8 minutes.
2. Add bell peppers and sauté for another 10 minutes or until tender.
3. Add black pepper, salt and tomato. Cook until tomato juice has evaporated, around 7 minutes.
4. Add olives, oregano and parsley, cook until heated through around 1 to 2 minutes. Transfer to a bowl and keep warm.
5. Wipe pan with paper towel and grease with cooking spray. Return to fire and place chicken breasts. Cook for three minutes per side or until desired doneness is reached. If needed, cook chicken in batches.
6. When cooking the last batch of chicken is done, add back the previous batch of chicken and the onion-bell pepper mixture and cook for a minute or two while tossing chicken to coat well in the onion-bell pepper mixture.
7. Serve and enjoy.

PER SERVING

Calories 261.8, Carb 11.0g, Protein36.0g, Fat 8.2g

Pork and Figs Mix

Prep time: 10 minutes | Cook time: 30 minutes| Serves 3

- 3 tablespoons avocado oil
- 1 and ½ pounds pork stew meat, roughly cubed
- Salt and black pepper to the taste
- 1 cup red onions, chopped
- 1 cup figs, dried and chopped
- 1 tablespoon ginger, grated
- 1 tablespoon garlic, minced
- 1 cup canned tomatoes, crushed
- 2 tablespoons parsley, chopped

1. Heat up a pot with the oil over medium-high heat, add the meat and brown for 5 minutes.
2. Add the onions and sauté for 5 minutes more.
3. Add the rest of the ingredients, bring to a simmer and cook over medium heat for 30 minutes more.
4. Divide the mix between plates and serve.

PER SERVING

Calories 309, fat 16, fiber 10.4, carbs 21.1, protein 34.2

Vegetarian Stew with Seitan

Prep time: 10 minutes| Cook time: 10 minutes| Serves 4

- ½ pound seitan, chopped
- 2 ½ cups vegetable broth
- 2 cloves garlic, minced
- 1 ½ carrots, peeled, chopped
- 2 medium potatoes, chopped
- 1 stalk celery, chopped
- freshly ground pepper, to taste
- 1 tomato, chopped
- 1 tablespoon soy sauce
- salt, to taste
- 2 tablespoons cornstarch mixed with 2 tablespoons of water
- 2 cloves garlic, peeled, minced
- olive oil, as required

1. This step is optional: Pour a little oil into a soup pot and let it heat over medium heat. Add seitan and stir. Cook for a few minutes.
2. Add garlic, and cook for a minute, or until fragrant. Add celery, potatoes, carrots, tomatoes, soy sauce, salt, and broth and stir.
3. Cook covered, until the vegetables are tender.
4. Add cornstarch mixture and stir constantly until thick.
5. Ladle into soup bowls and serve with whole-grain bread if desired. You can also serve it over brown rice or with a salad.

PER SERVING ¼ OF THE RECIPE, WITHOUT SERVING OPTIONS

Calories: 384,Fat: 1 g,Total carbohydrates: 80 g,Protein: 16 g

Chicken Fry with Peanut Sauce

Prep time: 10 minutes | Cook time: 15 minutes| Serves 4

- Meat from 4 chicken thighs, cut into bite-size pieces
- 2 tbsp. + ¼ cup peanut oil
- ½ cup peanut butter
- 3 tbsp. toasted sesame oil
- 2 tbsp. soy sauce
- 1 tbsp. lime juice
- 1 clove garlic, minced
- 1 tsp. powdered ginger
- 1-2 tsp. hot sauce, if desired
- 2 red bell peppers, chopped
- 2 tbsp. toasted sesame seeds
- 4 green onions, thinly sliced

1. Heat 2 tbsp. peanut oil in a large frying pan.
2. Add the chicken and cook for about 10 minutes, until no pink remains.
3. Meanwhile, mix together the peanut butter, ¼ cup peanut oil, sesame oil, soy sauce, lime juice, garlic, ginger, and hot sauce.
4. Add more water if needed to achieve a smooth consistency.
5. When the chicken is done, add the red pepper and cook for 1 minutes more.
6. Divide the chicken and peppers between four plates and top with peanut sauce, toasted sesame seeds, and green onions.

PER SERVING

Calories: :426.9 ,Sugars::4.8 g ,Total Carbohydrate :16.9 g ,Protein :38.7 g

Red Curry Quinoa Soup

Prep time: 10 minutes| Cook time: 20 minutes| Serves 3

- ½ tablespoon olive oil
- ½ green bell pepper, deseeded, chopped
- 1 clove garlic, chopped
- 1 teaspoon chopped fresh ginger
- ¼ yellow onion, chopped (about ⅓ cup)
- ¾ cup sweet potato, chopped
- ½ tablespoon red curry paste, or to taste
- ½ cup quinoa
- 1 tablespoon lime juice
- fresh cilantro, chopped, to garnish
- 2 cups vegetable broth or water
- salt, to taste

1. Pour oil into a pot and let it heat over medium-high heat. When the oil is hot, add onion, and cook for about 2 minutes. Stir in sweet potato and bell pepper.
2. Cook for about 10 minutes.
3. Stir in ginger, garlic, and curry paste. Stir constantly for about a minute or until you get a nice aroma. Make sure you do not burn the spices.
4. Add quinoa and stir fry for a minute.
5. Add broth and stir.
6. When it begins to boil, lower the heat and cook until sweet potatoes and quinoa are cooked.
7. Turn off the heat. Stir in lime juice and salt.
8. Ladle into soup bowls. Sprinkle cilantro on top and serve.

PER SERVING : OF THE RECIPE

Calories: 164,Fat: 4 g,Total carbohydrates: 26 g,Protein: 6 g

Pea Soup

Prep time: 8 minutes| Cook time: 10 minutes| Serves 8

- 2 onions, chopped
- 2 large potatoes, peeled, cubed
- 6 cups vegetable broth or water
- salt, to taste
- 2 tablespoons lemon juice
- pepper, to taste
- 2 large cloves garlic, peeled, sliced
- 1.3 pounds peas, fresh or frozen
- 2 tablespoons vegetable oil
- a handful fresh parsley or any other herbs of your choice, chopped
- To serve:
- ½ cup boiled peas
- vegan yogurt or vegan cream, or regular Greek yogurt to drizzle
- roasted chopped peanuts
- whole-grain bread

1. Pour oil into a soup pot and let it heat over medium heat. Add oil. When the oil is hot, add onion and garlic and cook until pink and soft.
2. Stir in the stock, salt, pepper, parsley, potatoes, and peas. When it begins to boil, lower the heat and cook covered until the potatoes are soft. Turn off the heat.
3. Blend with an immersion blender until smooth.
4. Add lemon juice and stir. Ladle into soup bowls. Serve with any of the suggested serving options.

PER SERVING OF THE RECIPE, WITHOUT SERV-ING OPTIONS

Calories: 182.9,Fat: 4.5 g,Total carbohydrates: 29.8 g,Protein: 5.6 g

Vegetable Soup

Prep time: 10 minutes| Cook time: 10 minutes| Serves 3

- ¾ teaspoon extra-virgin olive oil
- ½ large carrot, peeled, chopped
- ½ red bell pepper, chopped
- 2 cups water
- 5 fresh basil leaves, sliced
- ¼ teaspoon fine sea salt
- 1 tablespoon chopped fresh parsley, to garnish
- ½ medium yellow onion, diced
- 1 stalk celery, chopped
- 2 cloves garlic, peeled, minced
- 2 tablespoons chopped fresh oregano
- 1 sprig fresh thyme
- pepper, to taste
- 2 cups chopped kale leaves, discard hard stems and ribs before chopping
- salt, to taste

1. Pour oil into a soup pot and let it heat over medium-high heat.
2. When the oil is hot, add onion, celery, and carrot and cook for a few minutes, until the onion turns soft.
3. Stir in garlic and bell pepper and stir constantly for a few seconds until you get a nice aroma.
4. Stir in water, tomatoes, thyme, and salt. When it starts boiling, turn down the heat to medium-low heat and cook until the vegetables are tender.
5. Stir in kale and cook until kale turns limp.
6. Serve in bowls.

PER SERVING OF THE RECIPE

Calories: 120,Fat: 2 g,Total carbohydrates: 23 g,Protein: 6 g

Carrot and Lentil Soup

Prep time: 5–8 minutes| Cook time: 10 minutes| Serves 4

- 2 teaspoons cumin seeds
- 2 tablespoons olive oil
- ⅔ cup split red lentils, rinsed
- ½ cup milk
- ¼ teaspoon chili flakes
- 21 ounces carrots, peeled, coarsely chopped
- 2 ½ cups hot vegetable stock
- salt, to taste
- pepper, to taste
- Greek yogurt to serve

1. Toast the cumin in a large saucepan until you get a nice aroma. Add chili flakes and stir for a few seconds. Remove half the cumin mixture and keep it aside.
2. Add oil into the saucepan along with carrots, stock, lentils, and milk and let it come to a boil. Turn down the heat and cook until the lentils are soft.
3. Blend the soup until smooth. Stir in seasonings. Serve in bowls topped with yogurt and the retained cumin mixture.

PER SERVING ¼ OF THE RECIPE

Calories: 238,Fat: 7 g,Total carbohydrates: 34 g,Protein: 11 g

Chapter 8
Fish and Seafood

Salmon with Vegetables
Prep time: 10 minutes | Cook time: 15 minutes | Serves 4

- 2 tablespoons olive oil
- 2 carrots
- 1 head fennel
- 2 squashes
- ¼ onion
- 1-inch ginger
- 1 cup white wine
- 2 cups water
- 2 parsley sprigs
- 2 tarragon sprigs
- 6 oz. salmon fillets
- 1 cup cherry tomatoes
- 1 scallion

1. In your skillet, heat olive oil, add fennel, squash, onion, ginger, and carrot, and cook until vegetables are soft.
2. Add wine, water, and parsley and cook for another 4-5 minutes.
3. Season salmon fillets and place in the pan.
4. Cook for 5 minutes per side or until it is ready.
5. Transfer salmon to a bowl, spoon tomatoes and scallion around salmon and serve.

PER SERVING

Calories: 301kcal, Fat: 17g, Carbohydrates: 2g, Protein: 8g

Crispy Fish
Prep time: 5 minutes | Cook time: 15 minutes | Serves 4

4 thick fish fillets
¼ cup all-purpose flour
1 egg
1 cup bread crumbs
2 tablespoons vegetables
Lemon wedge

1. In a dish, add flour, egg, and breadcrumbs to different dishes and set aside.
2. Dip each fish fillet into the flour, egg, and then bread crumbs bowl.
3. Place each fish fillet in a heated skillet and cook for 4-5 minutes per side.
4. When ready, remove from pan and serve with lemon wedges.

PER SERVING

Calories: 189kcal, Fat: 17g, Carbohydrates: 2g, Protein: 7g

Moules Marinieres
Prep time: 10 minutes | Cook time: 30 minutes | Serves 4

- 2 tablespoons ghee
- 1 leek
- 1 shallot
- 2 cloves garlic
- 2 bay leaves
- 1 cup white win
- 2 lb. mussels
- 2 tablespoons mayonnaise
- 1 tablespoon lemon zest
- 2 tablespoons parsley
- 1 sourdough bread

1. In a saucepan, melt ghee, add leeks, garlic, bay leaves, and shallot and cook until vegetables are soft.
2. Bring to a boil, add mussels, and cook for 1-2 minutes.
3. Transfer mussels to a bowl and cover.
4. Whisk in the remaining ghee with mayonnaise and return the mussels to the pot.
5. Add lemon juice and parsley lemon zest and stir to combine.

PER SERVING

Calories: 321kcal, Fat: 17g, Carbohydrates: 2g, Protein: 9g

Steamed Mussels with Coconut-Curry
Prep time: 15 minutes | Cook time: 20 minutes | Serves 4

- 6 sprigs cilantro
- 2 cloves garlic
- 2 shallots
- ¼ teaspoon coriander seeds
- ¼ teaspoon red chili flakes
- 1 teaspoon zest
- 1 can of coconut milk
- 1 tablespoon vegetable oil
- 1 tablespoon curry paste
- 1 tablespoon brown sugar
- 1 tablespoon fish sauce
- 2 lb. mussels

1. Combine lime zest, cilantro stems, shallot, garlic, coriander seed, chili, and salt in a bowl.
2. In a saucepan, heat oil. Add garlic, shallots, pounded paste, and curry paste.
3. Cook for 3-4 minutes. Add coconut milk, sugar, and fish sauce.
4. Bring to a simmer and add mussels.
5. Stir in lime juice and cilantro leaves and cook for a few more minutes.
6. When ready, remove from heat and serve.

PER SERVING

Calories: 209kcal, Fat: 7g, Carbohydrates: 6g, Protein: 17g

Tuna Noodle Casserole

Prep time: 15 minutes | Cook time: 20 minutes | Serves 4

- 2 oz. egg noodles
- 4 oz. fraiche
- 1 egg
- 1 teaspoon cornstarch
- 1 tablespoon juice from 1 lemon
- 1 can tuna
- 1 cup peas
- ¼ cup parsley

1. Place noodles in a saucepan with water and bring to a boil.
2. Mix egg, crème fraiche, and lemon juice in a bowl, and whisk well.
3. When noodles are cooked, add the crème fraiche mixture to the skillet and mix well.
4. Add tuna, peas, parsley lemon juice, and mix well.
5. When ready, remove from heat and serve.

PER SERVING

Calories: 214kcal, Fat: 7g, Carbohydrates: 2g, Protein: 19g

Salmon Burgers

Prep time: 10 minutes | Cook time: 15 minutes | Serves 4

- 1 lb. salmon fillets
- 1 onion
- ¼ dill fronds
- 1 tablespoon honey
- 1 tablespoon horseradish
- 1 tablespoon mustard
- 1 tablespoon olive oil
- 2 toasted split rolls
- 1 avocado

1. Place salmon fillets in a blender and blend until smooth. Transfer to a bowl, add onion, dill, honey, and horseradish, and mix well.
2. Add salt and pepper and form 4 patties.
3. In a bowl, combine mustard, honey, mayonnaise, and dill.
4. In a skillet, heat oil, add salmon patties, and cook for 2-3 minutes per side.
5. When ready, remove from heat.
6. Divided lettuce and onion between the buns.
7. Place salmon patty on top and spoon mustard mixture and avocado slices.
8. Serve when ready.

PER SERVING

Calories: 189kcal, Fat: 7g, Carbohydrates: 6g, Protein: 12g

Seared Scallops

Prep time: 15 minutes | Cook time: 20 minutes | Serves 4

- 1 lb. sea scallops
- 1 tablespoon canola oil

1. Season scallops and refrigerate for a couple of minutes.
2. In a skillet, heat oil, add scallops, and cook for 1-2 minutes per side.
3. When ready, remove from heat and serve.

PER SERVING

Calories: 283kcal, Fat: 8g, Carbohydrates: 10g, Protein: 9g

Black Cod

Prep time: 15 minutes | Cook time: 20 minutes | Serves 4

- ¼ cup miso paste
- ¼ cup sake
- 1 tablespoon mirin
- 1 teaspoon soy sauce
- 1 tablespoon olive oil
- 4 black cod filets

1. Combine miso, soy sauce, oil, and sake in a bowl.
2. Rub mixture over cod fillets and let it marinade for 20-30 minutes.
3. Adjust broiler and broil cod filets for 10-12 minutes.
4. When fish is cooked, remove and serve.

PER SERVING

Calories: 213kcal, Fat: 15g, Carbohydrates: 2g, Protein: 8g

Miso-Glazed Salmon

Prep time: 10 minutes | Cook time: 40 minutes | Serves 4

- ¼ cup red miso
- ¼ cup sake
- 1 tablespoon soy sauce
- 1 tablespoon vegetable oil
- 4 salmon fillets

1. In a bowl, combine sake, oil, soy sauce, and miso.
2. Rub mixture over salmon fillets and marinade for 20-30 minutes.
3. Preheat a broiler.
4. Broil salmon for 5-10 minutes.
5. When ready, remove and serve.

PER SERVING

Calories: 198kcal, Fat: 10g, Carbohydrates: 5g, Protein: 6g

Salmon Pasta

Prep time: 10 minutes | Cook time: 25 minutes | Serves 2

- 5 tablespoons ghee
- ¼ onion
- 1 tablespoon all-purpose flour
- 1 teaspoon garlic powder
- 2 cups skim milk
- ¼ cup Romano cheese
- 1 cup green peas
- ¼ cup canned mushrooms
- 8 oz. salmon
- 1 package of penne pasta

1. Bring your pot with water to a boil.
2. Add pasta and cook for 10-12 minutes.
3. In a skillet, melt ghee, add onion and sauté until tender.
4. Stir in garlic powder, flour, milk, and cheese.
5. Add mushrooms and peas and cook on low heat for 4-5 minutes.
6. Toss in salmon and cook for another 2-3 minutes.
7. When ready, serve with cooked pasta.

PER SERVING

Calories: 211kcal, Fat: 18g, Carbohydrates:7 g, Protein: 17g

Chapter 9
Sides and Salads

Crispy Fennel Salad

Prep time: 5 minutes | Cook time: 15 minutes | Serves 2

- 1 fennel bulb, finely sliced
- 1 grapefruit, cut into segments
- 1 orange, cut into segments
- 2 tablespoons almond slices, toasted
- 1 teaspoon chopped mint
- 1 tablespoon chopped dill
- Salt and pepper to taste
- 1 tablespoon grape seed oil

1. Mix the fennel bulb with the grapefruit and orange segments on a platter.
2. Top with almond slices, mint and dill, drizzle with the oil, and season with salt and pepper.
3. Serve the salad as fresh as possible.

PER SERVING

Calories: 104Kcal, Fat: 0.5g, Carbohydrates: 25.5g, Protein: 3.1g

Provencal Summer Salad

Prep time: 5 minutes | Cook time: 25 minutes | Serves 2

- 1 zucchini, sliced
- 1 eggplant, sliced
- 2 red onions, sliced
- 2 tomatoes, sliced
- 1 teaspoon dried mint
- 2 garlic cloves, minced
- 2 tablespoons balsamic vinegar
- Salt and pepper to taste

1. Season the zucchini, eggplant, onions and tomatoes with salt and pepper. Cook the vegetable slices on the grill until browned.
2. Transfer the vegetables to a salad bowl, then add the mint, garlic and vinegar.
3. Serve the salad right away.

PER SERVING

Calories: 74Kcal, Fat: 0.5g, Carbohydrates: 16.5g, Protein: 3g

Roasted Vegetable Salad

Prep time: 5 minutes | Cook time: 30 minutes | Serves 6

- ½ pound of baby carrots
- 2 red onions, sliced
- 1 zucchini, sliced
- 2 eggplants, cubed
- 1 cauliflower, cut into florets
- 1 sweet potato, peeled and cubed
- 1 endive, sliced
- 3 tablespoons extra virgin olive oil
- 1 teaspoon dried basil
- Salt and pepper to taste
- 1 lemon, juiced
- 1 tablespoon balsamic vinegar

1. Combine the vegetables with the oil, basil, salt and pepper in a deep-dish baking pan and cook in the preheated oven at 350F for 25-30 minutes.
2. When done, transfer to a salad bowl and add the lemon juice and vinegar.
3. Serve the salad fresh.

PER SERVING

Calories: 164Kcal, Fat: 7.6g, Carbohydrates: 24.2g, Protein: 3.7g

Spanish Tomato Salad

Prep time: 5 minutes | Cook time: 10 minutes | Serves 2

- 1 pound of tomatoes, cubed
- 2 cucumbers, cubed
- 2 garlic cloves, chopped
- 1 red onion, sliced
- 2 anchovy fillets
- 1 tablespoon balsamic vinegar
- 1 pinch of chili powder
- Salt and pepper to taste

1. Combine the tomatoes, cucumbers, garlic and red onion in a bowl.
2. Mix the anchovy fillets, vinegar, chili powder, salt and pepper in a mortar.
3. Drizzle the mixture over the salad and mix well.
4. Serve the salad fresh.

PER SERVING

Calories: 61Kcal, Fat: 0.6g, Carbohydrates: 13g, Protein: 3g

Grilled Salmon Summer Salad

Prep time: 5 minutes | Cook time: 30 minutes | Serves 2

- 2 salmon fillets
- salt and pepper to taste
- 2 cups vegetable stock
- 1 2 cup bulgur
- 1 cup cherry tomatoes, halved
- 1 2 cup sweet corn
- 1 cucumber, cubed
- 1 green onion chopped
- 1 red bell pepper, cored and diced

1. Heat a grill pan on medium and then place salmon on, seasoning with salt and pepper. Grill both sides of salmon until brown and set aside.
2. Heat stock in a saucepan until hot, add in bulgur and cook until liquid is completely soaked into bulgur.
3. Mix salmon, bulgur, and all other ingredients in a salad bowl, and again add salt and pepper, if desired, to suit your taste.
4. Serve the salad as soon as completed.

PER SERVING

Calories: 60Kcal, Fat: 3g, Carbohydrates: 5g, Protein: 8g

Garden Salad with Oranges And Olives

Prep time: 5 minutes | Cook time: 10 minutes | Serves 2

- ½ cup red wine vinegar
- 1 tbsp extra virgin olive oil
- 1 tbsp finely chopped celery
- 1 tbsp finely chopped red onion
- 16 large ripe black olives
- 2 garlic cloves
- 2 navel oranges, peeled and segmented
- 4 boneless, skinless chicken breasts, 4 oz. each
- 4 garlic cloves, minced
- 8 cups leaf lettuce, washed and dried
- Cracked black pepper to taste

1. Prepare the dressing by mixing the pepper, celery, onion, olive oil, garlic and vinegar in a small bowl. Whisk well to combine.
2. Lightly grease the grate and preheat the grill to high.
3. Rub chicken with the garlic cloves and discard the garlic.
4. Grill chicken for 5 minutes per side or until cooked through.
5. Remove from grill and let it stand for 5 minutes before cutting into ½-inch strips.
6. On 4 serving plates, evenly arrange two cups of lettuce, ¼ of the sliced oranges and 4 olives per plate.
7. Top each dish with ¼ serving of grilled chicken, evenly drizzle with dressing, serve and enjoy.

PER SERVING

Calories: 259.8Kcal, Fat: 1.4g, Carbohydrates: 12.9g, Protein: 48.9g

Salmon & Arugula Salad

Prep time: 5 minutes | Cook time: 10 minutes | Serves 2

- ¼ cup red onion, sliced thinly
- 1 ½ tbsp fresh lemon juice
- 1 ½ tbsp olive oil
- 1 tbsp extra-virgin olive oil
- 1 tbsp red-wine vinegar
- 2 center-cut salmon fillets (6-oz each)
- 2/3 cup cherry tomatoes, halved
- 3 cups of baby arugula leaves
- Pepper and salt to taste

1. Mix pepper, salt, 1 ½ tbsp olive oil, and lemon juice in a shallow bowl. Toss in salmon fillets and rub with the marinade. Allow marinating for at least 15 minutes.
2. Grease a baking sheet and preheat the oven to 350ºF.
3. Bake marinated salmon fillet for 10 to 12 minutes or until flaky with skin side touching the baking sheet.
4. Meanwhile, in a salad bowl, mix onion, tomatoes, and arugula.
5. Season with pepper and salt. Drizzle with vinegar and oil. Toss to combine and serve right away with baked salmon on the side.

PER SERVING

Calories: 400Kcal, Fat: 25.6g, Carbohydrates: 5.8g, Protein: 36.6g

Chicken Salad

Prep time: 5 minutes | Cook time: 10 minutes | Serves 2

- 1 cup buffalo sauce
- 1 tablespoon honey
- 1 tsp lime
- 1 tsp salt
- 1 tsp onion powder
- 1 tablespoon olive oil
- 1 cup salad dressing

1. In a bowl, combine all ingredients and mix well.
2. Add dressing and serve.

PER SERVING

Calories: 44Kcal, Fat: 3g, Carbohydrates: 4.4g, Protein: 8.4g

Farro Salad

Prep time: 5 minutes | Cook time: 10 minutes | Serves 2

- 1 cup farro
- 1 bay leaf
- 1 shallot
- ¼ cup olive oil
- 1 tablespoon apple cider vinegar
- 1 tsp honey
- 1 cup arugula
- 1 apple
- ¼ cup basil
- ¼ cup parsley

1. In a bowl, combine all ingredients and mix well.
2. Add dressing and serve.

PER SERVING

Calories: 69Kcal, Fat: 6.5g, Carbohydrates: 10.6g, Protein: 9.4g

Carrot Salad

Prep time: 5 minutes | Cook time: 10 minutes | Serves 2

- 1 lb. carrots
- 1 cup raisins
- ½ cup peanuts
- ½ cup cilantro
- 2 green onions
- ¼ cup olive oil
- 1 tablespoon honey
- 2 cloves garlic
- 1 tsp cumin

1. In a bowl, combine all ingredients and mix well.
2. Add dressing and serve.

PER SERVING

Calories: 41Kcal, Fat: 6g, Carbohydrates: 9.6g, Protein: 11g

Warm Barley and Squash Salad with Balsamic Vinaigrette

Prep time: 20 minutes | Cook time: 40 minutes | Makes 8

- 1 small butternut squash, peeled and diced
- 3 teaspoons, plus 2 tablespoons extra-virgin olive oil, divided
- 2 cups broccoli florets
- 1 cup pearl barley
- 2 cups baby kale
- 1 cup toasted chopped walnuts
- ½ red onion, sliced
- 2 tablespoons balsamic vinegar
- 2 garlic cloves, minced
- ½ teaspoon salt
- ¼ teaspoon freshly ground black pepper

1. Preheat the oven to 400°F. Line a baking sheet with parchment paper.
2. In a large bowl, toss the squash with 2 teaspoons of olive oil. Transfer to the prepared baking sheet and roast for 20 minutes.
3. While the squash is roasting, toss the broccoli in the same bowl with 1 teaspoon of olive oil. After 20 minutes, flip the squash and push it to one side of the baking sheet. Add the broccoli to the other side and continue to roast for 20 minutes more until tender.
4. While the veggies are roasting, in a medium pot, cover the barley with several inches of water. Bring to a boil, then reduce the heat, cover, and simmer for 30 minutes until tender. Drain and rinse.
5. Transfer the barley to a large bowl and toss with the cooked squash and broccoli, kale, walnuts, and onion.
6. In a small bowl, mix the remaining 2 tablespoons of olive oil, the balsamic vinegar, garlic, salt, and pepper. Toss the salad with the dressing and serve.
7. Store in the refrigerator for up to 3 days or freeze in individual servings for up to 6 months.

PER SERVING (ABOUT 1½ CUPS)

Calories: 274; Protein: 6g; Total fat: 15g; Total carbohydrates: 32g; Fiber: 7g; Sugars: 3g; Sodium: 144mg; Iron: 2mg

Fattoush

Prep time: 10 minutes | Cook time: 10 minutes | Makes 8

- 4 whole-wheat pitas, chopped
- 2 tablespoons, plus ¼ cup extra-virgin olive oil
- 1 teaspoon lemon pepper, divided
- 1 head of butter lettuce, shredded
- 1 cucumber, chopped
- 1 pint cherry tomatoes, halved
- 1 bunch scallions, chopped
- 5 radishes, thinly sliced
- 3 tablespoons freshly squeezed lime juice
- ½ teaspoon sea salt
- ½ teaspoon ground cinnamon
- ¼ teaspoon ground allspice

1. Preheat the oven to 375°F. Line a baking sheet with parchment paper.
2. In a small bowl, mix the chopped pita with 2 tablespoons of olive oil and ½ teaspoon of lemon pepper. Mix well.
3. Spread in a single layer on the prepared baking sheet and bake in the oven until golden brown. Set aside to cool.
4. In a large bowl, combine the lettuce, cucumber, cherry tomatoes, scallions, and radishes.
5. Add the cooled pita bread and toss.
6. In a small bowl, whisk together the remaining ¼ cup of olive oil, ½ teaspoon of lemon pepper, the lime juice, salt, cinnamon, and allspice. Toss with the pita salad.
7. Store components separately. Store the pitas in a zip-top bag in a cupboard for up to 1 week. Store the salad tightly sealed in the refrigerator for up to 3 days. Store the dressing in a container in the refrigerator for up to 3 days. Toss all together to serve.

PER SERVING (ABOUT 2 CUPS)

Calories: 199; Protein: 4g; Total fat: 11g; Total carbohydrates: 23g; Fiber: 4g; Sugars: 3g; Sodium: 226mg; Iron: 2mg

Greek Salad

Prep time: 10 minutes | Makes 4

- 1 head butter lettuce
- 1 cucumber, chopped
- 1 pint cherry tomatoes, halved
- ½ red onion, thinly sliced
- ½ cup black olives, chopped
- ¼ cup crumbled feta cheese
- 4 servings Greek Lemon Vinaigrette

1. In a large bowl, combine the lettuce, cucumber, cherry tomatoes, onion, olives, and cheese. Mix.
2. Toss with the vinaigrette.
3. Store the dressing and salad separately, both in tightly sealed containers, in the refrigerator for up to 3 days. Toss before serving.

PER SERVING (ABOUT 2 CUPS)

Calories: 224; Protein: 4g; Total fat: 18g; Total carbohydrates: 2g; Fiber: 1g; Sugars: 0g; Sodium: 94mg; Iron: 1mg

Chicken Chopped Salad

Prep time: 10 minutes, plus 6 hours to marinate | Cook time: 25 minutes | Makes 4

- 2 boneless, skinless chicken breast halves
- 4 servings Greek Lemon Vinaigrette, divided
- 1 head romaine lettuce
- 2 Roma tomatoes, chopped
- 1 red bell pepper, seeded, ribs removed, and chopped
- 1 zucchini, chopped
- 1 bunch scallions, chopped
- ¼ cup plain Greek yogurt
- 2 garlic cloves, minced
- 1 tablespoon red wine vinegar

1. In a zip-top bag, marinate the chicken breasts in two servings of the vinaigrette for 6 hours or overnight.
2. Preheat the oven to 400°F. Remove the chicken breasts from the vinaigrette and pat them dry. Place on a rimmed baking sheet and cook in the oven for 20 to 25 minutes, until the chicken reaches an internal temperature of 165°F. Let cool, then chop into cubes.
3. In a large bowl, combine the chicken, lettuce, tomatoes, bell pepper, zucchini, and scallions. Mix.
4. In a smaller bowl, whisk together the remaining two servings of lemon vinaigrette, the Greek yogurt, garlic, and red wine vinegar. Toss with the salad.
5. Store the dressing and salad separately, both in tightly sealed containers, in the refrigerator for up to 3 days. Toss before serving.

PER SERVING (ABOUT 2 CUPS)

Calories: 132; Protein: 0g; Total fat: 14g; Total carbohydrates: 14g; Fiber: 5g; Sugars: 7g; Sodium: 316mg; Iron: 3mg

Oven-Roasted Eggplant Slices

Prep time: 5 minutes | Cook time: 30 minutes | Makes 4

- ¼ cup extra-virgin olive oil
- 1 teaspoon garlic powder
- 1 teaspoon Italian seasoning
- ½ teaspoon sea salt
- ¼ teaspoon freshly ground black pepper
- Pinch red pepper flakes (optional)
- 2 eggplants, cut into ½-inch-thick slices, unpeeled

1. Preheat the oven to 400°F. Line two rimmed baking sheets with parchment paper.
2. In a small bowl, whisk together the olive oil, garlic powder, Italian seasoning, salt, black pepper, and red pepper flakes.
3. Brush the mixture on both sides of the eggplant slices and place them in a single layer on the prepared baking sheets.
4. Bake in the oven until golden brown, 25 to 30 minutes.
5. Store in the refrigerator for up to 3 days.

PER SERVING (½ EGGPLANT)

Calories: 190; Protein: 3g; Total fat: 14g; Total carbohydrates: 17g; Fiber: 8g; Sugars: 10g; Sodium: 152mg; Iron: 1mg

Apple-Ginger Slaw

Prep time: 10 minutes | Makes 4

- 4 apples, peeled, cored, and julienned
- 1 fennel bulb, cored and julienned
- 1 tablespoon freshly squeezed lemon juice
- ½ cup plain Greek yogurt
- 1 tablespoon grated fresh ginger
- 1 teaspoon apple cider vinegar
- Pinch sea salt
- 1 teaspoon honey (optional)

1. In a large bowl, combine the apples and fennel. Toss with the lemon juice.
2. In a small bowl, whisk together the yogurt, ginger, vinegar, salt, and honey (if using).
3. Toss with the apples and fennel.
4. Store tightly sealed in the refrigerator for up to 3 days.

PER SERVING (½ CUP)

Calories: 134; Protein: 2g; Total fat: 1g; Total carbohydrates: 31g; Fiber: 6g; Sugars: 23g; Sodium: 85mg; Iron: 1mg

Ponzu Grilled Avocado

Prep time: 5 minutes | Cook time: 5 minutes | Makes 4

- 2 avocadoes, peeled and pitted
- 4 servings Easy Ponzu Sauce
- 1 tablespoon sesame seeds

1. Preheat a grill pan or grill on high.
2. Lightly brush the avocado halves on both sides with the ponzu sauce.
3. Place on the grill, cut-side down, and allow the grill to mark the avocado, 1 to 2 minutes. Turn the avocadoes over and mark the other side as well, another 1 to 2 minutes.
4. Put the avocadoes on plates and brush with the ponzu sauce. Fill the cavities with the remaining ponzu and sprinkle with the sesame seeds.
5. Store in zip-top bags in the refrigerator for up to 3 days.

PER SERVING (½ AVOCADO)

Calories: 203; Protein: 4g; Total fat: 16g; Total carbohydrates: 15g; Fiber: 7g; Sugars: 5g; Sodium: 648mg; Iron: 1mg

Crispy Roasted Brussels Sprouts with Pine Nuts

Prep time: 10 minutes | Cook time: 30 minutes | Makes 4

- 1½ pounds Brussels sprouts, halved and trimmed
- 2 tablespoons extra-virgin olive oil
- ½ teaspoon sea salt
- ¼ teaspoon freshly ground black pepper
- ¼ cup balsamic vinegar
- Juice and grated zest of ½ orange
- 1 tablespoon pure maple syrup
- 1 garlic clove, minced
- ¼ cup pine nuts

1. Preheat the oven to 400°F.
2. In a large bowl, toss the Brussels sprouts with the olive oil, salt, and pepper. Spread in a single layer on two rimmed baking sheets and roast in the oven until browned, 20 to 30 minutes.
3. While the Brussels sprouts are cooking, in a small saucepan, combine the balsamic vinegar, orange juice and zest, maple syrup, and garlic. Bring to a simmer over medium-high heat and simmer until thick and syrupy, about 10 minutes.
4. Put the roasted Brussels sprouts in a bowl. Toss with the pine nuts and the balsamic glaze.
5. Store leftovers in a zip-top bag in the refrigerator for up to 3 days.

PER SERVING (½ CUP)

Calories: 223; Protein: 7g; Total fat: 13g; Total carbohydrates: 24g; Fiber: 7g; Sugars: 10g; Sodium: 193mg; Iron: 3mg

Garlicky Green Beans

Prep time: 10 minutes | Cook time: 10 minutes | Makes 4

- 1 teaspoon sea salt
- 1 pound green beans, stemmed and halved
- 2 tablespoons extra-virgin olive oil
- 4 garlic cloves, minced
- Grated zest of 1 lemon

1. Bring a large pot of water to a boil and add the sea salt.
2. Add the green beans and boil for 5 minutes.
3. Strain into a colander and immediately run under cold water to stop the cooking. Drain.
4. In a large skillet, heat the olive oil over medium-high heat until it shimmers. Add the green beans and cook, stirring, for 3 minutes.
5. Add the garlic and cook, stirring constantly, for 30 seconds.
6. Remove from the heat and stir in the lemon zest.
7. Store in the refrigerator for up to 3 days or in the freezer for up to 6 months.

PER SERVING (½ CUP

Calories: 99; Protein: 2g; Total fat: 7g; Total carbohydrates: 9g; Fiber: 3g; Sugars: 4g; Sodium: 298mg; Iron: 1mg

Chili Lime Coleslaw

Prep time: 10 minutes | Makes 4

- 1 head cabbage, shredded
- 1 bunch scallions, thinly sliced
- ¼ cup chopped fresh cilantro
- 5 radishes, grated
- 1 carrot, grated
- Juice of 2 limes
- Grated zest of 1 lime
- ¼ cup extra-virgin olive oil
- ½ teaspoon Chinese hot mustard powder (optional)
- ½ teaspoon chipotle chili powder
- 1 teaspoon honey

1. In a large bowl, combine the cabbage, scallions, cilantro, radishes, and carrot. Mix.
2. In a small bowl, whisk together the lime juice and zest, olive oil, hot mustard powder (if using), chipotle chili powder, and honey. Toss with the slaw.
3. Store tightly sealed in the refrigerator for up to 3 days.

PER SERVING (½ CUP)

Calories: 201; Protein: 4g; Total fat: 14g; Total carbohydrates: 20g; Fiber: 7g; Sugars: 10g; Sodium: 68mg; Iron: 2mg

Chapter 10
Grain Recipes

Bell Peppers 'N Tomato-Chickpea Rice

Prep time: 10 minutes | Cook time: 35 minutes | Serves 4

- 2 tablespoons olive oil
- 1/2 chopped red bell pepper
- 1/2 chopped green bell pepper
- 1/2 chopped yellow pepper
- 1/2 chopped red pepper
- 1 medium onion, chopped
- 1 clove of garlic, minced
- 2 cups cooked jasmine rice
- 1 teaspoon tomato paste
- 1 cup chickpeas
- salt to taste
- 1/2 teaspoon paprika
- 1 small tomato, chopped
- Parsley for garnish

1. Whisk well olive oil, garlic, tomato paste, and paprika in a large mixing bowl. Season with salt generously.
2. Mix in rice and toss well to coat in the dressing.
3. Add remaining ingredients and toss well to mix.
4. Let salad rest to allow flavors to mix for 15 minutes.
5. Toss one more time and adjust the salt to taste if needed.
6. Garnish with parsley and serve.

PER SERVING

Calories: 490Kcal, Fat: 8.0g Carbohydrates: 93.0g, Protein: 10.0g

Fennel Wild Rice Risotto

Prep time: 5 minutes | Cook time: 35 minutes | Serves 6

- 2 tablespoons extra virgin olive oil
- 1 shallot, chopped
- 2 garlic cloves, minced
- 1 fennel bulb, chopped
- 1 cup wild rice
- ¼ cup dry white wine
- 2 cups chicken stock
- 1 teaspoon grated orange zest
- Salt and pepper to taste

1. Heat the oil in a heavy saucepan.
2. Add the garlic, shallot and fennel and cook for a few minutes until softened.
3. Stir in the rice and cook for 2 additional minutes, then add the wine, stock and orange zest, with salt and pepper to taste.
4. Cook on low heat for 20 minutes.
5. Serve the risotto warm and fresh.

PER SERVING

Calories: 162Kcal, Fat: 2g Carbohydrates: 20g, Protein: 8g

Wild Rice Prawn Salad

Prep time: 5 minutes | Cook time: 35 minutes | Serves 6

- ¾ cup wild rice
- 1¾ cups chicken stock
- 1 pound prawns
- Salt and pepper to taste
- 2 tablespoons lemon juice
- 2 tablespoons extra virgin olive oil
- 2 cups arugula

1. Combine the rice and chicken stock in a saucepan and cook until the liquid is absorbed.
2. Transfer the rice to a salad bowl.
3. Season the prawns with salt and pepper and drizzle them with lemon juice and oil.
4. Heat a grill pan over medium flame.
5. Place the prawns on the hot pan and cook on each side for 2-3 minutes.
6. For the salad, combine the rice with arugula and prawns and mix well.
7. Serve the salad fresh.

PER SERVING

Calories: 207Kcal, Fat: 4g Carbohydrates: 17g, Protein: 20.6g

Raspberry Overnight Porridge

Prep time: Overnight | Cook time: 0 minute | Serves12

- ⅓ cup of rolled oats
- ½ cup almond milk
- 1 tablespoon of honey
- 5-6 raspberries, fresh or canned and unsweetened
- ⅓ cup of rolled oats
- ½ cup almond milk
- 1 tablespoon of honey
- 5-6 raspberries, fresh or canned and unsweetened

1. Combine the oats, almond milk, and honey in a mason jar and place in the fridge overnight.
2. Serve the following day with the raspberries on top.

PER SERVING

Calories: 143.6Kcal, Fat: 3.91g Carbohydrates: 34.62g, Protein: 3.44g

Buckwheat and Grapefruit Porridge

Prep time: 5 minutes | Cook time: 20 minutes | Serves 2

- ½ cup buckwheat
- ¼ chopped grapefruit
- 1 tablespoon honey
- 1 ½ cup almond milk
- 2 cups water

1. Boil water on the stove. Add the buckwheat and place the lid on the pan.
2. Simmer for 7 to 10 minutes, in a low heat. Check to ensure water does not dry out.
3. Remove and set aside for 5 minutes, do this when most of the water is absorbed.
4. Drain excess water from the pan and stir in almond milk, heating through for 5 minutes.
5. Add the honey and grapefruit.
6. Serve.

PER SERVING

Calories: 231Kcal, Fat: 4g Carbohydrates: 43g, Protein: 24.2g

Cherry Berry Bulgur Bowl

Prep time: 15 minutes | Cook time: 15 minutes | Serves 4

- 1 cup medium-grind bulgur
- 2 cups water
- Pinch salt
- 1 cup halved and pitted cherries or 1 cup canned cherries, drained
- ½ cup raspberries
- ½ cup blackberries
- 1 tablespoon cherry jam
- 2 cups plain whole-milk yogurt

1. Mix the bulgur, water, and salt in a medium saucepan. Do this in medium heat. Bring to a boil.
2. Reduce the heat to low, then simmer, partially covered, for 12 to 15 minutes or until the bulgur is almost tender. Cover, and let stand for 5 minutes to finish cooking. Do this after removing the pan from the heat.
3. While the bulgur is cooking, combine the raspberries and blackberries in a medium bowl. Stir the cherry jam into the fruit.
4. When the bulgur is tender, divide it among four bowls. Top each bowl with ½ cup of yogurt and an equal amount of the berry mixture and serve.

PER SERVING

Calories: 242Kcal, Fat: 6g Carbohydrates: 44g, Protein: 9g

Baked Curried Apple Oatmeal Cups

Prep time: 10 minutes | Cook time: 20 minutes | Serves 6

- 3½ cups old-fashioned oats
- 3 tablespoons brown sugar
- 2 teaspoons of your preferred curry powder
- ⅛ teaspoon salt
- 1 cup unsweetened almond milk
- 1 cup unsweetened applesauce
- 1 teaspoon vanilla
- ½ cup chopped walnuts

1. Preheat the oven to 375°F.
2. Spray a 12-cup muffin tin with baking spray, then set aside.
3. Combine the oats, brown sugar, curry powder, and salt in a medium bowl.
4. Mix the milk, applesauce, and vanilla in a small bowl.
5. Stir the liquid ingredients into the dry ingredients and mix until just combined. Stir in the walnuts.
6. Divide the mixture among the muffin cups using a scant ⅓ cup for each.
7. Bake this for 18 to 20 minutes until the oatmeal is firm. Serve.

PER SERVING

Calories: 296Kcal, Fat: 10g Carbohydrates: 45g, Protein: 8g

Crunchy Quinoa Meal

Prep time: 5 minutes | Cook time: 25 minutes | Serves 2

- 3 cups coconut milk
- 1 cup rinsed quinoa
- 1/8 tsp. ground cinnamon
- 1 cup raspberry
- 1/2 cup chopped coconuts

1. In a saucepan, pour milk and bring to a boil over moderate heat.
2. Add the quinoa to the milk, and then bring it to a boil once more.
3. Then, let it simmer for at least 15 minutes on medium heat until the milk is reduced.
4. Stir in the cinnamon, then mix properly.
5. Cover it, then cook for 8 minutes until the milk is completely absorbed.
6. Add the raspberry and cook the meal for 30 seconds.
7. Serve and enjoy.

PER SERVING

Calories: 271Kcal, Fat: 3.7g Carbohydrates: 54g, Protein: 6.5g

Banana Quinoa

Prep time: 10 minutes | Cook time: 12 minutes | Serves 4

- 1 cup quinoa
- 2 cup milk
- 1 teaspoon vanilla extract
- 1 teaspoon honey
- 2 bananas, sliced
- ¼ teaspoon ground cinnamon

1. Pour milk into the saucepan and add quinoa.
2. Close the lid and cook it over medium heat for 12 minutes or until quinoa will absorb all liquid.
3. Chill the quinoa for about 10-15 minutes and place in the serving mason jars.
4. Add honey, vanilla extract, and ground cinnamon.
5. Stir well.
6. Top quinoa with banana and stir it before serving.

PER SERVING

Calories: 279Kcal, Fat: 5.3g Carbohydrates: 48.4g, Protein: 10.7g

Chapter 11
Snack

Strawberry Frozen Yogurt

Prep time: 10 minutes | Cook time: 15 minutes | Serves 4

- 15 ounces of plain yogurt
- 6 ounces of strawberries
- Juice of 1 orange
- 1 tablespoon honey

1. Place the strawberries and orange juice into a food processor or blender and blitz until smooth.
2. Press the mixture through a sieve into a large bowl to remove seeds.
3. Stir in the honey and yogurt. Transfer the mixture to an ice-cream maker and follow the manufacturer's instructions.
4. Alternatively, pour the mixture into a container and place in the fridge for 1 hour. Use a fork to whisk it and break up the ice crystals and freeze for 2 hours.

PER SERVING

Calories 238 ,Sodium 33 mg ,Dietary Fiber 1.4 g ,Total Fat 1.8 g ,Total Carbs 12.3 g ,Protein 1.3 g

Wheat Crackers

Prep time: 10 minutes | Cook time: 20 minutes | Serves 4

- 1 3/4 cups almond flour
- 1 1/2 cups coconut flour
- 3/4 teaspoon sea salt
- 1/3 cup vegetable oil
- 1 cup alkaline water
- Sea salt for sprinkling

1. Set your oven to 350 degrees F.
2. Mix coconut flour, almond flour and salt in a bowl.
3. Stir in vegetable oil and water. Mix well until smooth.
4. Spread this dough on a floured surface into a thin sheet.
5. Cut small squares out of this sheet.
6. Arrange the dough squares on a baking sheet lined with parchment paper.
7. Bake for 20 minutes until light golden in color.
8. Serve

PER SERVING

Calories 64 ,Total Fat 9.2 g ,Saturated Fat 2.4 g ,Cholesterol 110 mg ,Sodium 276 mg ,Total Carbs 9.2 g ,Fiber 0.9 g ,Sugar 1.4 g ,Protein 1.5 g

Oatmeal Cookies

Prep time: 10 minutes | Cook time: 30 minutes | Serves 3

- ¾ C. whole wheat flour
- 1 C. instant oats
- 1½ tsp. organic baking powder
- 1½ tsp. ground cinnamon
- 1/8 tsp. salt
- 1 large organic egg, room temperature
- ½ C. organic honey
- 2 tbsp. coconut oil, melted
- 1 tsp. organic vanilla extract
- 1 C. red apple, cored and chopped finely

1. In a large bowl, mix together flour, oats, baking powder, cinnamon and salt.
2. In another bowl, add remaining ingredients except apple and beat until well combined.
3. Add the flour mixture and mix until just combined.
4. Gently, fold in the apple.
5. Refrigerate for about 30 minutes.
6. Preheat the oven to 325 degrees F. Line a large baking sheet with parchment paper.
7. Place about 2 tbsp. of the mixture onto the preparation ared baking sheet in the shape of small mounds.
8. With the back of a spoon, flatten each cookie slightly
9. Bake for about 13-15 minutes.
10. Cool on the pan for 10 minutes before turning out onto a wire rack.
11. Remove from oven and keep onto a wire rack to cool for about 5 minutes.
12. Carefully invert the cookies onto the wire rack to cool completely before serving

PER SERVING

Calories448, fat 27g , carbs41g, protein15g

Trail Mix

Prep time: 10 minutes | Cook time: 10 minutes | Serves 3

- ¼ cup unsalted roasted peanuts
- ¼ cup whole shelled almonds
- ¼ cup chopped pitted dates
- ¼ cup dried cranberries
- 2 ounces dried apricots

1. In a medium bowl, mix together all the ingredients until well combined. Enjoy!

PER SERVING

Calories448 ,fat27g , carbs41g , protein 41g

Yogurt Dip

Prep time: 10 minutes | Cook time: 10 minutes| Serves 5

- 2 cups Greek yogurt
- 2 tablespoons pistachios, toasted and chopped
- A pinch of salt and white pepper
- 2 tablespoons mint, chopped
- 1 tablespoon kalamata olives, pitted and chopped
- ¼ cup za'atar spice
- ¼ cup pomegranate seeds
- 1/3 cup olive oil

1. In a bowl, combine the yogurt with the pistachios and the rest of the ingredients, whisk well, divide into small cups and serve with pita chips on the side.

PER SERVING

Calories 91, fat 5.1, fiber 3, carbs 3, protein 4.3

Eggplant Dip

Prep time: 10 minutes | Cook time: 40 minutes| Serves 3

- 1 eggplant, poked with a fork
- 2 tablespoons tahini paste
- 2 tablespoons lemon juice
- 2 garlic cloves, minced
- 1 tablespoon olive oil
- Salt and black pepper to the taste
- 1 tablespoon parsley, chopped

1. Put the eggplant in a roasting pan, bake at 400 degrees F for 40 minutes, cool down, peel and transfer to your food processor.
2. Add the rest of the ingredients except the parsley, pulse well, divide into small bowls and serve as an appetizer with the parsley sprinkled on top.

PER SERVING

Calories 121, fat 4.3, fiber 1, carbs 1.4, protein 4.3

Zucchini Cakes

Prep time: 10 minutes | Cook time: 10 minutes| Serves 4

- 1 zucchini, grated
- ¼ carrot, grated
- ¼ onion, minced
- 1 teaspoon minced garlic
- 3 tablespoons coconut flour
- 1 teaspoon Italian seasonings
- 1 egg, beaten
- 1 teaspoon coconut oil

1. In the mixing bowl combine together grated zucchini, carrot, minced onion, and garlic.
2. Add coconut flour, Italian seasoning, and egg.
3. Stir the mass until homogenous.
4. Heat up coconut oil in the skillet.
5. Place the small zucchini fritters in the hot oil. Make them with the help of the spoon.

6. Roast the zucchini fritters for 4 minutes from each side.

PER SERVING

Calories 65, fat 3.3, fiber 3, carbs 6.3, protein 3.3

Honey Garlic Shrimp

Prep time: 10 minutes | Cook time: 5 minutes| Serves 3

- 1 lb shrimp, peeled and deveined
- 1/4 cup honey
- 1 tbsp garlic, minced
- 1 tbsp ginger, minced
- 1 tbsp olive oil
- 1/4 cup fish stock
- Pepper
- Salt

1. Add shrimp into the large bowl. Add remaining ingredients over shrimp and toss well.
2. Transfer shrimp into the instant pot and stir well.
3. Seal pot with lid and cook on high for 5 minutes.
4. Once done, release pressure using quick release. Remove lid.
5. Serve and enjoy.

PER SERVING

Calories 240, Fat 5.6 g, Carbohydrates 20.9 g, Sugar 17.5 g, Protein 26.5 g, Cholesterol 239 mg

Cucumber-basil Salsa On Halibut Pouches

Prep time: 10 minutes | Cook time: 20 minutes| Serves 3

- 1 lime, thinly sliced into 8 pieces
- 2 cups mustard greens, stems removed
- 2 tsp olive oil
- 4 – 5 radishes trimmed and quartered
- 4 4-oz skinless halibut filets
- 4 large fresh basil leaves
- Cayenne pepper to taste – optional
- Pepper and salt to taste
- 1 ½ cups diced cucumber
- 1 ½ finely chopped fresh basil leaves
- 2 tsp fresh lime juice
- Pepper and salt to taste

1. Preheat oven to 400oF.
2. Preparation are parchment papers by making 4 pieces of 15 x 12-inch rectangles. Lengthwise, fold in half and unfold pieces on the table.
3. Season halibut fillets with pepper, salt and cayenne—if using cayenne.
4. Just to the right of the fold going lengthwise, place ½ cup of mustard greens. Add a basil leaf on center of mustard greens and topped with 1 lime slice. Around the greens, layer ¼ of the radishes. Drizzle with ½ tsp of oil, season with pepper and salt. Top it with a slice of halibut fillet.
5. Just as you would make a calzone, fold parchment paper over your filling and crimp the edges of the parchment paper beginning from one end to the other end. To seal the end of the crimped parchment paper, pinch it.
6. Repeat process to remaining ingredients until you have 4 pieces of parchment papers filled with halibut and greens.
7. Place pouches in a baking pan and bake in the oven until halibut is flaky, around 15 to 17 minutes.
8. While waiting for halibut pouches to cook, make your salsa by mixing all salsa ingredients in a medium bowl.
9. Once halibut is cooked, remove from oven and make a tear on top. Be careful of the steam as it is very hot. Equally divide salsa and spoon ¼ of salsa on top of halibut through the slit you have created.
10. Serve and enjoy.

PER SERVING

Calories 335.4, Protein20.2g, Fat 16.3g, Carbs 22.1g

Black-Eyed Peas Spread

Prep time: 10 minutes| Cook time: 30 minutes| Serves 8

- 8 ounces plain, fat-free Greek yogurt
- 1 tablespoon chopped fresh chives
- ¼ teaspoon sea salt
- ½ can (from a 14 ounce can) quartered artichokes, rinsed, drained
- 1 cup chopped green onion (optional)
- ¼ cup light mayonnaise
- ½ clove garlic, peeled, minced
- ½ can (from a 15 ounce can) black-eyed peas, rinsed, drained, lightly mashed
- ¼ cup shredded mozzarella cheese
- 4 cups cucumber slices or celery sticks

1. Preheat the oven to 350°F. Prepare a small pie pan or small baking dish by greasing it with cooking spray.
2. Add mayonnaise, yogurt, chives, salt, and garlic into a bowl and mix well.
3. Add artichoke hearts and black-eyed peas and mix well. Spread this mixture on the pie plate.
4. Scatter cheese on top and put the pie pan into the oven. Set the timer for about 25 minutes or until the cheese melts and browns at a few spots.
5. Let it rest for 10 minutes. Garnish with green onions.
6. Serve cucumber slices with black-eyed peas spread.

PER SERVING ½ CUP CUCUMBER SLICES WITH 3 TABLESPOONS OF SPREAD

Calories: 78,Fat: 3 g,Total carbohydrates: 9 g,Protein: 4 g

Feta Tomato Sea Bass

Prep time: 10 minutes | Cook time: 10 minutes| Serves 3

- 4 sea bass fillets
- 1 1/2 cups water
- 1 tbsp olive oil
- 1 tsp garlic, minced
- 1 tsp basil, chopped
- 1 tsp parsley, chopped
- 1/2 cup feta cheese, crumbled
- 1 cup can tomatoes, diced
- Pepper
- Salt

1. Season fish fillets with pepper and salt.
2. Pour 2 cups of water into the instant pot then place steamer rack in the pot.
3. Place fish fillets on steamer rack in the pot.
4. Seal pot with lid and cook on high for 5 minutes.
5. Once done, release pressure using quick release. Remove lid.
6. Remove fish fillets from the pot and clean the pot.
7. Add oil into the inner pot of instant pot and set the pot on sauté mode.
8. Add garlic and sauté for 1 minute.
9. Add tomatoes, parsley, and basil and stir well and cook for 1 minute.
10. Add fish fillets and top with crumbled cheese and cook for a minute.
11. Serve and enjoy.

PER SERVING

Calories 219, Fat 10.1 g, Carbohydrates 4 g, Sugar 2.8 g, Protein 27.1 g, Cholesterol 70 mg

Jalapeno Chickpea Hummus

Prep time: 10 minutes | Cook time: 20 minutes| Serves 3

- 1 cup dry chickpeas, soaked overnight and drained
- 1 tsp ground cumin
- 1/4 cup jalapenos, diced
- 1/2 cup fresh cilantro
- 1 tbsp tahini
- 1/2 cup olive oil
- Pepper
- Salt

1. Add chickpeas into the instant pot and cover with vegetable stock.
2. Seal pot with lid and cook on high for 25 minutes.
3. Once done, allow to release pressure naturally. Remove lid.
4. Drain chickpeas well and transfer into the food processor along with remaining ingredients and process until smooth.
5. Serve and enjoy.

PER SERVING

Calories 425, Fat 30.4 g, Carbohydrates 31.8 g, Sugar 5.6 g, Protein 10.5 g, Cholesterol 0 mg

Kale Chips

Prep time: 10 minutes | Cook time: 5 minutes| Serves 3

- 1 lb. fresh kale leaves, stemmed and torn
- ¼ tsp. cayenne pepper
- Salt, to taste
- 1 tbs. olive oil

1. Preheat the oven to 350 degrees F. Line a large baking sheet with a parchment paper.
2. Place the kale pieces onto preparation ared baking sheet in a single layer.
3. Sprinkle the kale with cayenne and salt and drizzle with oil.
4. Bake for about 10-15 minutes.

PER SERVING

Calories242, carbs25g, fat 12g, protein 13g

Avocado Dip

Prep time: 10 minutes | Cook time: 10 minutes| Serves 8

- ½ cup heavy cream
- 1 green chili pepper, chopped
- Salt and pepper to the taste
- 4 avocados, pitted, peeled and chopped
- 1 cup cilantro, chopped
- ¼ cup lime juice

1. In a blender, combine the cream with the avocados and the rest of the ingredients and pulse well.
2. Divide the mix into bowls and serve cold as a party dip.

PER SERVING

Calories 200, fat 14.5, fiber 3.8, carbs 8.1, protein 7.6

Chicken Bites

Prep time: 10 minutes | Cook time: 5 minutes| Serves 5

- ½ cup coconut flakes
- 8 oz chicken fillet
- ¼ cup Greek yogurt
- 1 teaspoon dried dill
- 1 teaspoon salt
- 1 teaspoon ground black pepper
- 1 tablespoon tomato sauce
- 1 teaspoon honey
- 4 tablespoons sunflower oil

1. Chop the chicken fillet on the small cubes (popcorn cubes)
2. Sprinkle them with dried dill, salt, and ground black pepper.
3. Then add Greek yogurt and stir carefully.
4. After this, pour sunflower oil in the skillet and heat it up.
5. Coat chicken cubes in the coconut flakes and roast in the hot oil for 3-4 minutes or until the popcorn cubes are golden brown.
6. Dry the popcorn chicken with the help of the paper towel.
7. Make the sweet sauce: whisk together honey and tomato sauce.
8. Serve the popcorn chicken hot or warm with sweet sauce.

PER SERVING

Calories 107, fat 5.2, fiber 0.8, carbs 2.8, protein 12.1

Lime Pea Guacamole

Prep time: 10 minutes | Cook time: 10 minutes| Serves 3

- 2 cups thawed frozen green peas
- ¼ cup fresh lime juice
- 1 teaspoon crushed garlic
- ½ teaspoon cumin
- 1/8 teaspoon hot sauce
- ½ cup chopped cilantro
- 4 green onions, chopped
- 1 tomato, chopped
- Black pepper

1. In a food processor, blend together peas, lime juice, garlic, and cumin until very smooth; transfer to a large bowl and stir in hot sauce, cilantro, green onion, tomato and pepper.
2. Refrigerate, covered, for about 30 minutes for flavors to blend. Enjoy!

PER SERVING

Calories324, fat 24g, protein20g, carbs7g

Red Pepper Tapenade

Prep time: 10 minutes | Cook time: 10 minutes| Serves 3

- 7 ounces roasted red peppers, chopped
- ½ cup parmesan, grated
- 1/3 cup parsley, chopped
- 14 ounces canned artichokes, drained and chopped
- 3 tablespoons olive oil
- ¼ cup capers, drained
- 1 and ½ tablespoons lemon juice
- 2 garlic cloves, minced

1. In your blender, combine the red peppers with the parmesan and the rest of the ingredients and pulse well.
2. Divide into cups and serve as a snack.

PER SERVING

Calories 200, fat 5.6, fiber 4.5, carbs 12.4, protein 4.6

Lemon Swordfish

Prep time: 10 minutes | Cook time: 30 minutes| Serves 2

- 12 oz swordfish steaks (6 oz every fish steak)
- 1 teaspoon ground cumin
- 1 tablespoon lemon juice
- ¼ teaspoon salt
- 1 teaspoon olive oil

1. Sprinkle the fish steaks with ground cumin and salt from each side.
2. Then drizzle the lemon juice over the steaks and massage them gently with the help of the fingertips.
3. Preheat the grill to 395F.
4. Bruhs every fish steak with olive oil and place in the grill.
5. Cook the swordfish for 3 minutes from each side.

PER SERVING

Calories 289, fat 1.4, fiber 0.1, carbs 0.6, protein 43.4

Plum Wraps

Prep time: 10 minutes | Cook time: 10 minutes| Serves 3

- 4 plums
- 4 prosciutto slices
- ¼ teaspoon olive oi

1. Preheat the oven to 375F.
2. Wrap every plum in prosciutto slice and secure with a toothpick (if needed).
3. Place the wrapped plums in the oven and bake for 10 minutes.

PER SERVING

Calories 62, fat 2.2, fiber 0.9, carbs 8, protein 4.3

Crunchy Veggie Chips

Prep time: 10 minutes | Cook time: 17 minutes| Serves 3

- 1 cup thinly sliced portobello mushrooms
- 1 cup thinly sliced zucchini
- 1 cup thinly sliced sweet potatoes
- 1 tablespoon extra-virgin olive oil
- Pinch of sea salt
- Pinch of pepper

1. Place veggies in a baking dish and drizzle with olive oil; sprinkle with salt and pepper and toss to coat well; bake at 325°F for about 12 minutes or until crunchy. Enjoy!

PER SERVING

Calories 448 , fat27g, carbs41g , protein 15g

Feta and Roasted Red Pepper Bruschetta

Prep time: 10 minutes | Cook time: 15 minutes| Serves 8

- 6 Kalamata olives, pitted, chopped
- 2 tablespoons green onion, minced
- 1/4 cup Parmesan cheese, grated, divided
- 1/4 cup extra-virgin olive oil brushing, or as needed
- 1/4 cup cherry tomatoes, thinly sliced
- 1 teaspoon lemon juice
- 1 tablespoon extra-virgin olive oil
- 1 tablespoon basil pesto
- 1 red bell pepper, halved, seeded
- 1 piece (12 inch) whole-wheat baguette, cut into 1/2-inch thick slices
- 1 package (4 ounce) feta cheese with basil and sun-dried tomatoes, crumbled
- 1 clove garlic, minced

1. Preheat the oven broiler. Place the oven rack 6 inches from the source of heat.
2. Brush both sides of the baguette slices, with the 1/4 cup olive oil. Arrange the bread slices on a baking sheet; toast for about 1 minute each side, carefully watching to avoid burning. Remove the toasted slices, transferring into another baking sheet.
3. With the cut sides down, place the red peppers in a baking sheet; broil for about 8 to 10 minutes or until the skin is charred and blistered. Transfer the roasted peppers into a bowl; cover with plastic wrap. Let cool, remove the charred skin. Discard skin and chop the roasted peppers.
4. In a bowl, mix the roasted red peppers, cherry tomatoes, feta cheese, green onion, olives, pesto, 1 tablespoon olive oil, garlic, and lemon juice.
5. Top each bread with 1 tablespoon of the roasted pepper mix, sprinkle lightly with the Parmesan cheese.
6. Return the baking sheet with the topped bruschetta; broil for about 1-2 minutes or until the topping is lightly browned.

PER SERVING

Cal73, total fat 4.8 g, sodium 138 mg, total carbs 5.3 g, fiber 0.4 g, sugar0.6 g, protein2.1 g

Vegetable Platter with Tzatziki Dip

Prep time: 10 minutes| Cook time: 20 minutes| Serves 3

- For vegetable platter:
- 3 cups water
- ½ head broccoli, cut into bite size pieces
- ½ watermelon radish, cut into thin round slices
- 1½ medium assorted colored carrots, cut into batons
- 1 cup cherry tomatoes
- ⅛ sea salt
- ½ bunch radish, cut into bite size pieces
- ½ cup sugar snap peas
- 3 stalks celery, cut into 1 ½ inch sticks
- 2 small assorted colored bell peppers, cut into about ⅓ inch wide, long pieces
- For tzatziki:
- ¼ cup shredded cucumber
- ¼ cup nonfat plain Greek yogurt
- ½ clove garlic, peeled, minced
- freshly ground pepper, to taste
- ½ teaspoon paprika, to garnish
- ⅛ teaspoon sea salt
- ½ teaspoon extra-virgin olive oil
- juice of ½ lemon
- 1 teaspoon chopped fresh dill, to garnish

1. To make the vegetable platter: Add about a teaspoon of salt to a pot of water and place it over medium-high heat.
2. When water starts boiling, drop the broccoli, watermelon radish, radish, carrots, and sugar snap peas into the pot and let it cook for exactly 3 minutes.
3. Have a large bowl of ice water nearby. Take out the broccoli, watermelon radish, radish broccoli, and sugar snap peas with a slotted spoon and drop them into the bowl of ice water.
4. Let the carrots cook in the boiling water for another 2 minutes. Take out the carrots and drop them into a bowl of ice water. Turn off the heat.
5. Let the vegetables cool completely. Drain in a colander. Dry the vegetables by patting with a kitchen towel.
6. Arrange celery, bell peppers, cherry tomatoes, boiled vegetables on a serving platter, in any colorful manner you desire.
7. Meanwhile, make the tzatziki dip: Combine salt and cucumber in a strainer. Let it drain for 10 minutes.
8. Add Greek yogurt, garlic, pepper, oil, and lemon juice into a blender and blend until smooth.
9. Pour into a bowl. Add cucumber and mix well. Garnish with paprika and dill.
10. Serve with vegetables.

PER SERVING

Calories: 93,Fat: 1 g,Total carbohydrates: 18 g,Protein: 6 g

Roasted Buffalo Chickpeas

Prep time: 5 minutes| Cook time: 30 minutes| Serves 2

- ½ tablespoon white vinegar
- ⅛ teaspoon salt
- ¼ teaspoon cayenne pepper, or to taste
- ½ can(from a 15 ounce can) unsalted chickpeas, drained, rinsed or ½ cup cooked unsalted chickpeas

1. Place the rack in the upper third position in the oven. Preheat the oven to 400°F.
2. Spread chickpeas over layers of paper towels. Dry the chickpeas by patting with more paper towels.
3. Add vinegar, cayenne pepper, and salt into a bowl. Add the chickpeas. Toss well.
4. Transfer on to a rimmed baking sheet and spread it evenly.
5. Place the baking sheet in the oven and set the timer for about 25–35 minutes or until crisp and brown.
6. Let it remain in the oven for 10 minutes. Remove from the oven and let it cool for 30 minutes.
7. Serve.

PER SERVING ¼ CUP

Calories: 109,Fat: 1 g,Total carbohydrates: 18 g,Protein: 6 g

Oatmeal Energy Balls

Prep time: 10 minutes + chilling time| Cook time: 10 minutes| Serves 10

- ½ cup old fashioned oats
- ⅓ cup smooth, natural peanut butter
- ¼ cup mini semi-sweet chocolate chips
- ½ teaspoon ground cinnamon
- ¼ cup ground flaxseeds
- 1½ tablespoons honey
- ½ teaspoon pure vanilla extract
- ½ teaspoon chia seeds (optional)

1. Combine oats, peanut butter, chocolate chips, cinnamon, flaxseeds, honey, vanilla, and chia seeds in a bowl.
2. Cover the bowl and chill for a couple of hours.
3. Divide the mixture into 10 equal portions and shape into balls.
4. You can serve it right away or transfer into an airtight container. It can last for a week.

PER SERVING 1 BALL

Calories: 150,Fat: 9 g,Total carbohydrates: 14 g,Protein: 5 g

Zucchini Fritters

Prep time: 15 minutes| Cook time: 35 minutes| Serves 5

- ½ cup buttermilk
- ¼ cup panko breadcrumbs
- ⅛ cup grated Parmesan cheese
- ⅛ teaspoon garlic salt
- ⅛ cup fat-free sour cream
- ⅛ cup salsa
- ⅛ cup egg substitute
- ¼ cup seasoned breadcrumbs
- ¾ teaspoon taco seasoning, or to taste
- 1½ medium zucchinis, cut into ¼ inch thick slices
- ⅛ cup fat-free ranch salad dressing

1. Preheat the oven to 400°F. Prepare a baking sheet by spraying some cooking spray.
2. Whisk together egg substitute and buttermilk in a bowl.
3. Add panko breadcrumbs, seasoned breadcrumbs, taco seasoning, cheese, and garlic salt into a shallow bowl and mix well.
4. Working with one zucchini slices at a time; dunk the slices in buttermilk mixture. Shake off extra mixture and dredge in the breadcrumb mixture.
5. Place the breaded zucchini slices on the baking sheet. Place the baking sheet in the oven and set the timer for about 25 minutes or until golden brown. Turn the zucchini slices over after about 12–14 minutes of baking.
6. Meanwhile, add ranch dressing, sour cream, and salsa into a bowl. Cover and set aside until the fritters are baked.
7. Serve zucchini fritters with sauce.

PER SERVING : CUP ZUCCHINI WITH A TABLE-SPOON OF SAUCE

Calories: 67,Fat: 1 g,Total carbohydrates: 11 g,Protein: 3 g

Appendix 1 Measurement Conversion Chart

Volume Equivalents (Dry)	
US STANDARD	**METRIC (APPROXIMATE)**
1/8 teaspoon	0.5 mL
1/4 teaspoon	1 mL
1/2 teaspoon	2 mL
3/4 teaspoon	4 mL
1 teaspoon	5 mL
1 tablespoon	15 mL
1/4 cup	59 mL
1/2 cup	118 mL
3/4 cup	177 mL
1 cup	235 mL
2 cups	475 mL
3 cups	700 mL
4 cups	1 L

Volume Equivalents (Liquid)		
US STANDARD	**US STANDARD (OUNCES)**	**METRIC (APPROXIMATE)**
2 tablespoons	1 fl.oz.	30 mL
1/4 cup	2 fl.oz.	60 mL
1/2 cup	4 fl.oz.	120 mL
1 cup	8 fl.oz.	240 mL
1 1/2 cup	12 fl.oz.	355 mL
2 cups or 1 pint	16 fl.oz.	475 mL
4 cups or 1 quart	32 fl.oz.	1 L
1 gallon	128 fl.oz.	4 L

Temperatures Equivalents	
FAHRENHEIT(F)	**CELSIUS(C) APPROXIMATE)**
225 °F	107 °C
250 °F	120 ° °C
275 °F	135 °C
300 °F	150 °C
325 °F	160 °C
350 °F	180 °C
375 °F	190 °C
400 °F	205 °C
425 °F	220 °C
450 °F	235 °C
475 °F	245 °C
500 °F	260 °C

Weight Equivalents	
US STANDARD	**METRIC (APPROXIMATE)**
1 ounce	28 g
2 ounces	57 g
5 ounces	142 g
10 ounces	284 g
15 ounces	425 g
16 ounces (1 pound)	455 g
1.5 pounds	680 g
2 pounds	907 g

Appendix 2 The Dirty Dozen and Clean Fifteen

The Environmental Working Group (EWG) is a nonprofit, nonpartisan organization dedicated to protecting human health and the environment Its mission is to empower people to live healthier lives in a healthier environment. This organization publishes an annual list of the twelve kinds of produce, in sequence, that have the highest amount of pesticide residue-the Dirty Dozen-as well as a list of the fifteen kinds ofproduce that have the least amount of pesticide residue-the Clean Fifteen.

THE DIRTY DOZEN	
The 2016 Dirty Dozen includes the following produce. These are considered among the year's most important produce to buy organic:	
Strawberries	Spinach
Apples	Tomatoes
Nectarines	Bell peppers
Peaches	Cherry tomatoes
Celery	Cucumbers
Grapes	Kale/collard greens
Cherries	Hot peppers

The Dirty Dozen list contains two additional itemskale/collard greens and hot peppers-because they tend to contain trace levels of highly hazardous pesticides.

THE CLEAN FIFTEEN	
The least critical to buy organically are the Clean Fifteen list. The following are on the 2016 list:	
Avocados	Papayas
Corn	Kiw
Pineapples	Eggplant
Cabbage	Honeydew
Sweet peas	Grapefruit
Onions	Cantaloupe
Asparagus	Cauliflower
Mangos	

Some of the sweet corn sold in the United States are made from genetically engineered (GE) seedstock. Buy organic varieties of these crops to avoid GE produce.

Appendix 3 Index

TRACY J. FREEMAN

Printed in Great Britain
by Amazon

13600286R00052